TREASURY OF
Easter Celebrations

The people who love Christ are set apart like the soft, glorious Pleiades that keep together in the sky.

Storm Jameson

TREASURY OF
Easter Celebrations

by Julie Hogan

IDEALS PUBLICATIONS
NASHVILLE, TENNESSEE

ISBN 0-8249-4206-X

Copyright © 1999 by Ideals Publications, a division of Guideposts

Library of Congress has already catalogued this book as follows:
Hogan, Julie, 1949–
    A treasury of Easter celebrations / by Julie Hogan. -- 1st ed.
    p.   cm.
    Includes index.
    1. Easter. 2. Easter--Poetry. 3. Easter stories. I. Title.
GT4935.H59   1999
394.2667--dc21   99-11812
                                                        CIP

Caseside printed in the U.S.A.
Text printed and bound in Mexico.
Printed by R.R. Donnelley & Sons.

The paper used in this publication meets the minimum requirements of American National Standard for Information Sciences—Permanence of Paper for Printed Library Materials, ANSI Z39, 48-1984.

Publisher, Patricia A. Pingry
Designer, Eve DeGrie
Copy Editor, Amy Johnson

Cover photograph: Sunrise over New London, New Hampshire. William H. Johnson/Johnson's Photography.

Color Separations by Precision Color Graphics, Franklin, Wisconsin.

Published by Ideals Publications, a division of Guideposts
535 Metroplex Drive, Suite 250
Nashville, Tennessee 37211

10 8 6 4 2 1 3 5 7 9

Photography Credits

Half-title page: Sunrise over White Mountain National Forest, New Hampshire. William H. Johnson/Johnson's Photography. Title page: Sunrise over Milan Hill State Park, New Hampshire. William H. Johnson/Johnson's Photography. Page 6: Church in Santorini, Greece. Suzanne and Nick Geary/Tony Stone Images. Page 38: Sunrise over Shenandoah National Park, Virginia. Hardie Truesdale/International Stock. Page 52: Sunrise over York, Maine. William H. Johnson/Johnson's Photography. Page 64: Sunrise over New London, New Hampshire. William H. Johnson/Johnson's Photography. Page 78: Lake of the Clouds, Mt. Washington, New Hampshire. William H. Johnson/Johnson's Photography. Page 104: Sunrise over Santa Rosa Island, Florida. William H. Johnson/Johnson's Photography.

Acknowledgments

BARTH, EDNA. Excerpts from *Lilies, Rabbits and Painted Eggs: The Story of the Easter Symbols* by Edna Barth. Text copyright ©1970 by Edna Barth. Reprinted by permission of Clarion Books/Houghton Mifflin Company. All rights reserved. BORLAND, HAL. Excerpt from *Borland Country*. Reprinted by permission of Frances Collin, Literary Agent. Copyright © 1947, 1948, 1949, 1950, 1951, 1952, 1953, 1955, 1956, 1971 by Hal Borland. COATSWORTH, ELIZABETH. "Easter." Reprinted by permission of Katherine Barnes. CORATHIEL, ELISABETHE H. C. Excerpt from *Oberammergau and Its Passion Play*, © 1970. Reprinted by permission of Paulist Press. DEVLIN, DENIS. Lines from "Ascension" by Denis Devlin from *Denis Devlin: Collected Poems*, J. C. C Mays, ed. With Permission of Wake Forest University Press. FARJEON, ELEANOR. "Morning Has Broken." Reprinted by permission of Harold Ober Associates Incorporated. Copyright 1951 by Eleanor Farjeon. Copyright renewed. FERGUSON, GEORGE. "Butterfly, Eagle, Egg, Lion, Aspen, Dandelion, Gourd, Grapes." Reproduced from *Signs and Symbols in Christian Art* by George Ferguson. Reprinted with the permission of Phaidon Press Limited. FOLEY, DANIEL. Excerpts from *Easter the World Over* by Priscilla Sawyer Lord and Daniel J. Foley. Reprinted by permission of Daniel J. Foley. FROST, ROBERT. "A Prayer in Spring" from *Collected Poems of Robert Frost*, ©1930 by Henry Holt and Company, Inc. Reprinted by permission of the publisher. GARIEPY, HENRY. Excerpts from *Songs in the Night: Inspiring Stories Behind 100 Hymns Born in Trial and Suffering*, © 1996 Wm. B. Eerdmans Publishing Co. Used by permission. HARTMAN, RACHEL. Excerpt from *The Joys of Easter* by Rachel Hartman. Copyright © Rachel Hartman, 1967. Reprinted by arrangement of Dutton Plume, a division of Penguin Putnam Inc.

JENKINS, EMYL. Excerpt from *The Book of American Traditions* by Emyl Jenkins. Copyright © 1996 by Emyl Jenkins. Reprinted by permission of Crown Publishers, Inc. MARSHALL, PETER. "With Sorrow and True Repentance" from *The Prayers of Peter Marshall*, compiled and edited by Caroline Marshall, copyright © 1949, 1950, 1951, 1954 by Catherine Marshall. Renewed 1982. Published by Chosen Books, a division of Baker Book House. Used by Permission. MARTIN, PAT. Excerpt from *Czechoslovak Culture, Recipes, History, and Folk Arts*. Reprinted by permission of Penfield Press. NICHOLSON, NORMAN. "The Ride to Jerusalem" from *Five Rivers* by Norman Nicholson. Copyright © 1945 by E. P. Dutton. Used by permission of Dutton, a division of Penguin Putnam Inc. SMITH, ETHEL. "Were You There When They Crucified My Lord?," "He Shall Feed His Flock," "For God So Loved the World," and "The Holy City." Music copyright 1952 by Ethel Smith Music Corp. International copyright secured. All rights reserved. Used by permission of Copyright Owner. THOMPSON, SUE ELLEN. Excerpt from *Holiday Symbols*. Reprinted by permission of Omnigraphics, Inc.

    Our sincere thanks to the following authors whom we were unable to locate: Gail Chase for an excerpt from *The Eye and the Eyebrow: A History of Kas, Turkey and Castellorizo*; Madeleine Sweeny Miller for "An Olive Tree Speaks"; and Elizabeth Hough Sechrist and Janette Woolsey for excerpts from *It's Time for Easter*.

    All possible care has been taken to fully acknowledge the ownership and use of every selection in this book. If any mistakes or omissions have occurred inadvertently, they will be corrected in subsequent editions, provided notification is sent to the publisher. Many of the poems included are traditional, with the author unknown.

CONTENTS

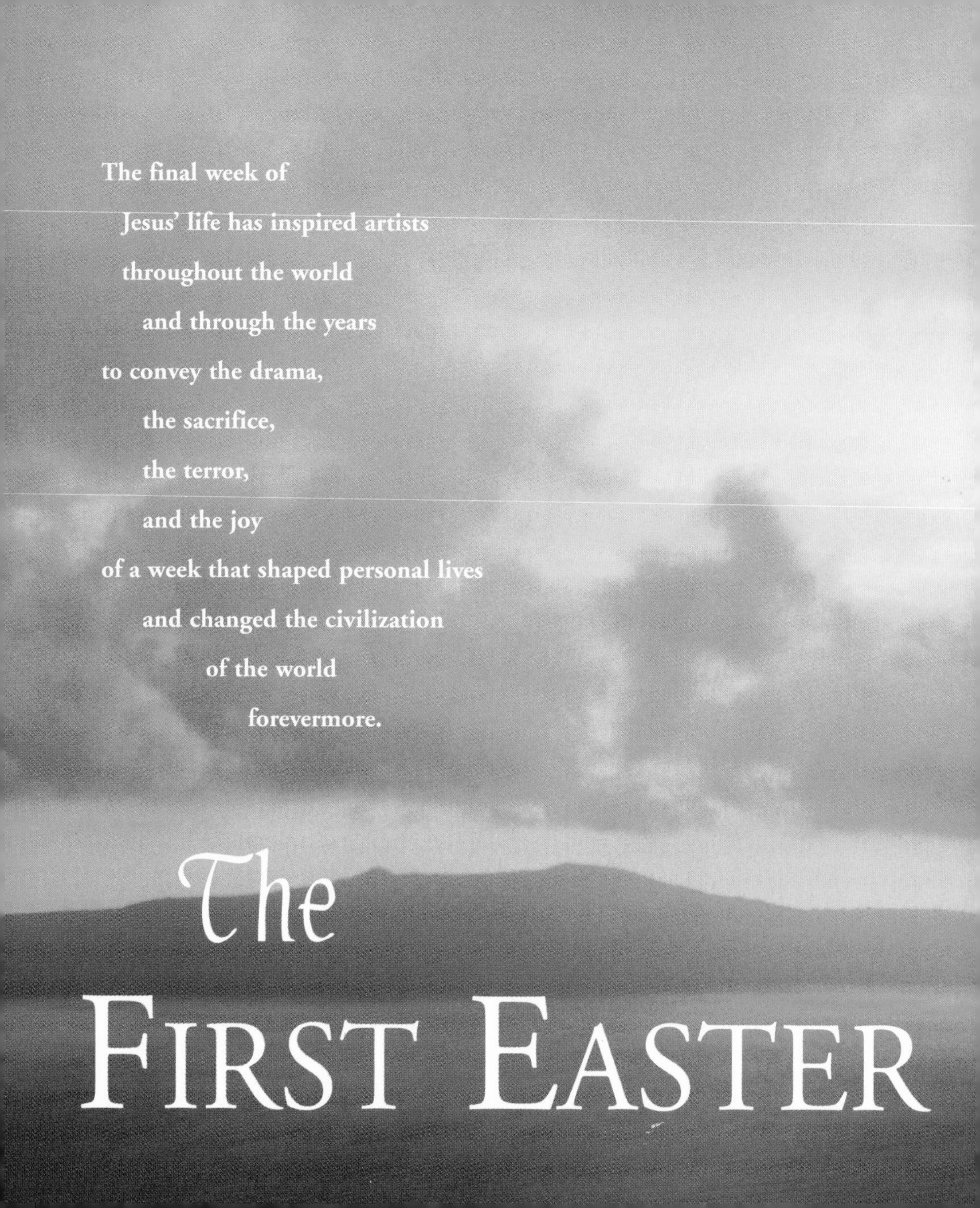

The final week of

Jesus' life has inspired artists

throughout the world

and through the years

to convey the drama,

the sacrifice,

the terror,

and the joy

of a week that shaped personal lives

and changed the civilization

of the world

forevermore.

The

FIRST EASTER

The Prophecy

Who hath believed our report? and to whom is the arm of the LORD revealed? For he shall grow up before him as a tender plant, and as a root out of a dry ground: he hath no form nor comeliness; and when we shall see him, there is no beauty that we should desire him. He is despised and rejected of men; a man of sorrows, and acquainted with grief: and we hid as it were our faces from him; he was despised, and we esteemed him not. Surely he hath borne our griefs, and carried our sorrows: yet we did esteem him stricken, smitten of God, and afflicted. But he was wounded for our transgressions, he was bruised for our iniquities: the chastisement of our peace was upon him; and with his stripes we are healed. All we like sheep have gone astray; we have turned every one to his own way; and the LORD hath laid on him the iniquity of us all. He was oppressed, and he was afflicted, yet he opened not his mouth: he is brought as a lamb to the slaughter, and as a sheep before her shearers is dumb, so he openeth not his mouth. He was taken from prison and from judgment: and who shall declare his generation? for

he was cut off out of the land of the living: for the transgression of my people was he stricken. And he made his grave with the wicked, and with the rich in his death; because he had done no violence, neither was any deceit in his mouth. Yet it pleased the LORD to bruise him; he hath put him to grief: when thou shalt make his soul an offering for sin, he shall see his seed, he shall prolong his days, and the pleasure of the LORD shall prosper in his hand.

Isaiah 53:1–10

THE PROPHET ISAIAH
Sixteenth Century Unknown Artist
Novgorod, Russia
Leonid Bogdanov/SuperStock

THE GOOD SHEPHERD
Philippe de Champaigne
Musée des Beaux-Arts, Lille, France
Giraudon/Art Resource, NY

The Triumphant Entry into Jerusalem

nd when he had thus spoken, he went before, ascending up to Jerusalem. And it came to pass, when he was come nigh to Bethphage and Bethany, at the mount called the mount of Olives, he sent two of his disciples, Saying, Go ye into the village over against you; in the which at your entering ye shall find a colt tied, whereon yet never man sat: loose him, and bring him hither. And if any man ask you, Why do ye loose him? thus shall ye say unto him, Because the Lord hath need of him.

And they that were sent went their way, and found even as he had said unto them. And as they were loosing the colt, the owners thereof said unto them, Why loose ye the colt?

And they said, The Lord hath need of him. And they brought him to Jesus: and they cast their garments upon the colt, and they set Jesus thereon.

And as he went, they spread their clothes in the way. And when he was come nigh, even now at the descent of the mount of Olives, the whole multitude of the disciples began to rejoice and praise God with a loud voice for all the mighty works that they had seen; Saying, Blessed be the King that cometh in the name of the Lord: peace in heaven, and glory in the highest.

And some of the Pharisees from among the multitude said unto him, Master, rebuke thy disciples. And he answered and said unto them, I tell you that, if these should hold their peace, the stones would immediately cry out. And when he was come near, he beheld the city, and wept over it.

Luke 19:28–41

THE TRIUMPHANT ENTRY INTO JERUSALEM
Santi di Tito
Accademia, Florence, Italy
Alinari/Art Resource, NY

Cleansing the Temple

And when he was come into Jerusalem, all the city was moved, saying, Who is this? And the multitude said, This is Jesus the prophet of Nazareth of Galilee. And Jesus went into the temple of God, and cast out all them that sold and bought in the temple, and overthrew the tables of the moneychangers, and the seats of them that sold doves,

And said unto them, It is written, My house shall be called the house of prayer; but ye have made it a den of thieves.

And the blind and the lame came to him in the temple; and he healed them. And when the chief priests and scribes saw the wonderful things that he did, and the children crying in the temple, and saying, Hosanna to the son of David; they were sore displeased,

And said unto him, Hearest thou what these say? And Jesus saith unto them, Yea; have ye never read, Out of the mouth of babes and sucklings thou hast perfected praise?

And he left them, and went out of the city into Bethany; and he lodged there.

Now in the morning as he returned into the city, he hungered.

And when he saw a fig tree in the way, he came to it, and found nothing thereon, but leaves only, and said unto it, Let no fruit grow on thee henceforward for ever. And presently the fig tree withered away. And when the disciples saw it, they marvelled, saying, How soon is the fig tree withered away!

Jesus answered and said unto them, Verily I say unto you, If ye have faith, and doubt not, ye shall not only do this which is done to the fig tree, but also if ye shall say unto this mountain, Be thou removed, and be thou cast into the sea; it shall be done. And all things, whatsoever ye shall ask in prayer, believing, ye shall receive.

Matthew 21:10–22

CHRIST CLEANSING THE TEMPLE
Carl Heinrich Bloch
SuperStock

The Last Supper

And the disciples did as Jesus had appointed them; and they made ready the passover. Now when the even was come, he sat down with the twelve. And as they did eat, he said, Verily I say unto you, that one of you shall betray me. And they were exceeding sorrowful, and began every one of them to say unto him, Lord, is it I?

And he answered and said, He that dippeth his hand with me in the dish, the same shall betray me. The Son of man goeth as it is written of him: but woe unto that man by whom the Son of man is betrayed! it had been good for that man if he had not been born.

Then Judas, which betrayed him, answered and said, Master, is it I?

He said unto him, Thou hast said. And as they were eating, Jesus took bread, and blessed it, and brake it, and gave it to the disciples, and said, Take, eat; this is my body.

And he took the cup, and gave thanks, and gave it to them, saying, Drink ye all of it; For this is my blood of the new testament, which is shed for many for the remission of sins. But I say unto you, I will not drink henceforth of this fruit of the vine, until that day when I drink it new with you in my Father's kingdom.

Matthew 26:19–29

THE LAST SUPPER
Leonardo da Vinci
S. Maria delle Grazie, Milan, Italy
Scala/Art Resource, NY

The Washing of the Feet

And supper being ended, the devil having now put into the heart of Judas Iscariot, Simon's son, to betray him; Jesus knowing that the Father had given all things into his hands, and that he was come from God, and went to God; He riseth from supper, and laid aside his garments; and took a towel, and girded himself. After that he poureth water into a basin, and began to wash the disciples' feet, and to wipe them with the towel wherewith he was girded.

Then cometh he to Simon Peter: and Peter saith unto him, Lord, dost thou wash my feet? Jesus answered and said unto him, What I do thou knowest not now; but thou shalt know hereafter.

Peter saith unto him, Thou shalt never wash my feet. Jesus answered him, If I wash thee not, thou hast no part with me. Simon Peter saith unto him, Lord, not my feet only, but also my hands and my head.

Jesus saith to him, He that is washed needeth not save to wash his feet, but is clean every whit: and ye are clean, but not all. For he knew who should betray him; therefore said he, Ye are not all clean. So after he had washed their feet, and had taken his garments, and was set down again, he said unto them, Know ye what I have done to you? Ye call me Master and Lord: and ye say well; for so I am. If I then, your Lord and Master, have washed your feet; ye also ought to wash one another's feet. For I have given you an example, that ye should do as I have done to you. Verily, verily, I say unto you, The servant is not greater than his lord; neither he that is sent greater than he that sent him. If ye know these things, happy are ye if ye do them. . . .

A new commandment I give unto you, That ye love one another; as I have loved you, that ye also love one another. By this shall all men know that ye are my disciples, if ye have love one to another.

John 13:2–17, 34–35

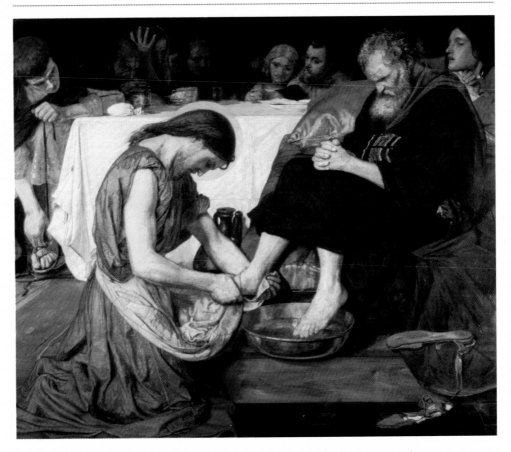

Jesus saith unto him, I am the way, the truth, and the life: no man cometh unto the Father, but by me.

John 14:6

CHRIST WASHING PETER'S FEET
Ford Madox Brown
Tate Gallery, London/Art Resource, NY

The Agony

And when they had sung an hymn, they went out into the mount of Olives. Then saith Jesus unto them, All ye shall be offended because of me this night: for it is written, I will smite the shepherd, and the sheep of the flock shall be scattered abroad. But after I am risen again, I will go before you into Galilee. . . .

Then cometh Jesus with them unto a place called Gethsemane, and saith unto the disciples, Sit ye here, while I go and pray yonder. And he took with him Peter and the two sons of Zebedee, and began to be sorrowful and very heavy.

Then saith he unto them, My soul is exceeding sorrowful, even unto death: tarry ye here, and watch with me.

And he went a little farther, and fell on his face, and prayed, saying, O my Father, if it be possible, let this cup pass from me: nevertheless not as I will, but as thou wilt.

And he cometh unto the disciples, and findeth them asleep, and saith unto Peter, What, could ye not watch with me one hour? Watch and pray, that ye enter not into temptation: the spirit indeed is willing, but the flesh is weak. He went away again the second time, and prayed, saying, O my Father, if this cup may not pass away from me, except I drink it, thy will be done.

And he came and found them asleep again: for their eyes were heavy. And he left them, and went away again, and prayed the third time, saying the same words.

Then cometh he to his disciples, and saith unto them, Sleep on now, and take your rest: behold, the hour is at hand, and the Son of man is betrayed into the hands of sinners.

Rise, let us be going: behold, he is at hand that doth betray me.

Matthew 26:30–32, 36–46

CHRIST IN THE GARDEN
Johann Liss
Christie's Images/SuperStock

The Betrayal

And while he yet spake, lo, Judas, one of the twelve, came, and with him a great multitude with swords and staves, from the chief priests and elders of the people. Now he that betrayed him gave them a sign, saying, Whomsoever I shall kiss, that same is he: hold him fast. And forthwith he came to Jesus, and said, Hail, master; and kissed him. And Jesus said unto him, Friend, wherefore art thou come? Then came they, and laid hands on Jesus, and took him.

And, behold, one of them which were with Jesus stretched out his hand, and drew his sword, and struck a servant of the high priest's, and smote off his ear.

Then said Jesus unto him, Put up again thy sword into his place: for all they that take the sword shall perish with the sword. Thinkest thou that I cannot now pray to my Father, and he shall presently give me more than twelve legions of angels? But how then shall the scriptures be fulfilled, that thus it must be? In that same hour said Jesus to the multitudes, Are ye come out as against a thief with swords and staves for to take me? I sat daily with you teaching in the temple, and ye laid no hold on me. But all this was done, that the scriptures of the prophets might be fulfilled. Then all the disciples forsook him, and fled.

And they that had laid hold on Jesus led him away to Caiaphas the high priest, where the scribes and the elders were assembled. . . . But Jesus held his peace. And the high priest answered and said unto him, I adjure thee by the living God, that thou tell us whether thou be the Christ, the Son of God. Jesus saith unto him, Thou hast said: nevertheless I say unto you, Hereafter shall ye see the Son of man sitting on the right hand of power, and coming in the clouds of heaven.

Matthew 26:47–57, 63–64

THE BETRAYAL
Anton van Dyck
The Prado, Madrid
Scala/Art Resource, NY

Peter Denies Jesus

But Peter followed him afar off unto the high priest's palace, and went in, and sat with the servants, to see the end. Now the chief priests, and elders, and all the council, sought false witness against Jesus, to put him to death; But found none: yea, though many false witnesses came, yet found they none. . . .

Then the high priest rent his clothes, saying, He hath spoken blasphemy; what further need have we of witnesses? behold, now ye have heard his blasphemy. What think ye? They answered and said, He is guilty of death. Then did they spit in his face, and buffeted him; and others smote him with the palms of their hands, Saying, Prophesy unto us, thou Christ, Who is he that smote thee?

Now Peter sat without in the palace: and a damsel came unto him, saying, Thou also wast with Jesus of Galilee. But he denied before them all, saying, I know not what thou sayest.

And when he was gone out into the porch, another maid saw him, and said unto them that were there, This fellow was also with Jesus of Nazareth.

And again he denied with an oath, I do not know the man. And after a while came unto him they that stood by, and said to Peter, Surely thou also art one of them; for thy speech bewrayeth thee.

Then began he to curse and to swear, saying, I know not the man. And immediately the cock crew. And Peter remembered the word of Jesus, which said unto him, Before the cock crow, thou shalt deny me thrice. And he went out, and wept bitterly.

Matthew 26:58–60, 65–75

THE DENIAL OF PETER
Rembrandt van Rijn
Rijksmuseum, Amsterdam
SuperStock

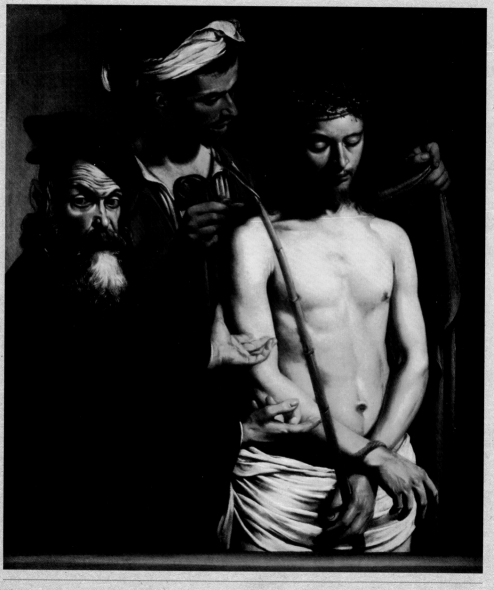

The Interrogation of Christ

And the Lord turned, and looked upon Peter. And Peter remembered the word of the Lord, how he had said unto him, Before the cock crow, thou shalt deny me thrice. And Peter went out, and wept bitterly.

And the men that held Jesus mocked him, and smote him. And when they had blindfolded him, they struck him on the face, and asked him, saying, Prophesy, who is it that smote thee? And many other things blasphemously spake they against him.

And as soon as it was day, the elders of the people and the chief priests and the scribes came together, and led him into their council, saying, Art thou the Christ? tell us.

And he said unto them, If I tell you, ye will not believe: And if I also ask you, ye will not answer me, nor let me go. Hereafter shall the Son of man sit on the right hand of the power of God.

Then said they all, Art thou then the Son of God?

And he said unto them, Ye say that I am.

And they said, What need we any further witness? for we ourselves have heard of his own mouth. And the whole multitude of them arose, and led him unto Pilate.

And they began to accuse him, saying, We found this fellow perverting the nation, and forbidding to give tribute to Caesar, saying that he himself is Christ a King.

And Pilate asked him, saying, Art thou the King of the Jews?

And he answered him and said, Thou sayest it. Then said Pilate to the chief priests and to the people, I find no fault in this man.

Luke 22:61–71, 23:1–4

THE INTERROGATION OF CHRIST
Caravaggio
Palazzo Rosso, Genoa, Italy
Scala/Art Resource, NY

The Trial of Jesus

And the chief priests accused him of many things: but he answered nothing. And Pilate asked him again, saying, Answerest thou nothing? behold how many things they witness against thee. But Jesus yet answered nothing; so that Pilate marvelled.

Now at that feast he released unto them one prisoner, whomsoever they desired. And there was one named Barabbas, which lay bound with them that had made insurrection with him, who had committed murder in the insurrection. And the multitude crying aloud began to desire him to do as he had ever done unto them.

But Pilate answered them, saying, Will ye that I release unto you the King of the Jews? For he knew that the chief priests had delivered him for envy. But the chief priests moved the people, that he should rather release Barabbas unto them. And Pilate answered and said again unto them, What will ye then that I shall do unto him whom ye call the King of the Jews?

And they cried out again, Crucify him. Then Pilate said unto them, Why, what evil hath he done? And they cried out the more exceedingly, Crucify him.

And so Pilate, willing to content the people, released Barabbas unto them, and delivered Jesus, when he had scourged him, to be crucified. And the soldiers led him away into the hall, called Praetorium; and they call together the whole band. And they clothed him with purple, and plaited a crown of thorns, and put it about his head, And began to salute him, Hail, King of the Jews! And they smote him on the head with a reed, and did spit upon him, and bowing their knees worshipped him. And when they had mocked him, they took off the purple from him, and put his own clothes on him, and led him out to crucify him.

Mark 15:3–20

THE FLAGELLATION OF CHRIST
Caravaggio
S. Domenico Maggiore, Naples, Italy
Scala/Art Resource, NY

The Crucifixion

And they bring him unto the place Golgotha, which is, being interpreted, The place of a skull. And they gave him to drink wine mingled with myrrh: but he received it not. And when they had crucified him, they parted his garments, casting lots upon them, what every man should take. And it was the third hour, and they crucified him. And the superscription of his accusation was written over, THE KING OF THE JEWS.

And with him they crucify two thieves; the one on his right hand, and the other on his left. And the scripture was fulfilled, which saith, And he was numbered with the transgressors. And they that passed by railed on him, wagging their heads, and saying, Ah, thou that destroyest the temple, and buildest it in three days, Save thyself, and come down from the cross. Likewise also the chief priests mocking said among themselves with the scribes, He saved others; himself he cannot save. Let Christ the King of Israel descend now from the cross, that we may see and believe. And they that were crucified with him reviled him.

And when the sixth hour was come, there was darkness over the whole land until the ninth hour. And at the ninth hour Jesus cried with a loud voice, saying, Eloi, Eloi, lama sabachthani? which is, being interpreted, My God, my God, why hast thou forsaken me? And some of them that stood by, when they heard it, said, Behold, he calleth Elias. And one ran and filled a spunge full of vinegar, and put it on a reed, and gave him to drink, saying, Let alone; let us see whether Elias will come to take him down. And Jesus cried with a loud voice, and gave up the ghost. And the veil of the temple was rent in twain from the top to the bottom. And when the centurion, which stood over against him, saw that he so cried out, and gave up the ghost, he said, Truly this man was the Son of God.

Mark 15:22–39

THE CRUCIFIXION OF JESUS CHRIST
Bartolomeo Esteban Murillo
The Prado, Madrid, Spain
Scala/Art Resource, NY

The Resurrection of Jesus Christ

And now when the even was come, because it was the preparation, that is, the day before the sabbath, Joseph of Arimathaea, an honourable counsellor, which also waited for the kingdom of God, came, and went in boldly unto Pilate, and craved the body of Jesus. And Pilate marvelled if he were already dead: and calling unto him the centurion, he asked him whether he had been any while dead.

And when he knew it of the centurion, he gave the body to Joseph. And he bought fine linen, and took him down, and wrapped him in the linen, and laid him in a sepulchre which was hewn out of a rock, and rolled a stone unto the door of the sepulchre. And Mary Magdalene and Mary the mother of Joses beheld where he was laid.

And when the sabbath was past, Mary Magdalene, and Mary the mother of James, and Salome, had bought sweet spices, that they might come and anoint him. And very early in the morning the first day of the week, they came unto the sepulchre at the rising of the sun. And they said among themselves, Who shall roll us away the stone from the door of the sepulchre? And when they looked, they saw that the stone was rolled away: for it was very great. And entering into the sepulchre, they saw a young man sitting on the right side, clothed in a long white garment; and they were affrighted.

And he saith unto them, Be not affrighted: Ye seek Jesus of Nazareth, which was crucified: he is risen; he is not here: behold the place where they laid him. But go your way, tell his disciples and Peter that he goeth before you into Galilee: there shall ye see him, as he said unto you. And they went out quickly, and fled from the sepulchre; for they trembled and were amazed: neither said they any thing to any man; for they were afraid.

Mark 15:42–47, 16:1–8

THE RESURRECTION OF CHRIST
Noel Coypel
Musée des Beaux-Arts, Rennes, France
Giraudon/Art Resource, NY

The Appearance

ary Magdalene came and told the disciples that she had seen the Lord, and that he had spoken these things unto her. Then the same day at evening, being the first day of the week, when the doors were shut where the disciples were assembled for fear of the Jews, came Jesus and stood in the midst, and saith unto them, Peace be unto you.

And when he had so said, he shewed unto them his hands and his side. Then were the disciples glad, when they saw the Lord.

Then said Jesus to them again, Peace be unto you: as my Father hath sent me, even so send I you. And when he had said this, he breathed on them, and saith unto them, Receive ye the Holy Ghost:

Whose soever sins ye remit, they are remitted unto them; and whose soever sins ye retain, they are retained.

But Thomas, one of the twelve, called Didymus, was not with them when Jesus came. The other disciples therefore said unto him, We have seen the Lord. But he said unto them, Except I shall see in his hands the print of the nails, and put my finger into the print of the nails, and thrust my hand into his side, I will not believe. And after eight days again his disciples were within, and Thomas with them: then came Jesus, the doors being shut, and stood in the midst, and said, Peace be unto you. Then saith he to Thomas, Reach hither thy finger, and behold my hands; and reach hither thy hand, and thrust it into my side: and be not faithless, but believing.

And Thomas answered and said unto him, My Lord and my God.

Jesus saith unto him, Thomas, because thou hast seen me, thou hast believed: blessed are they that have not seen, and yet have believed.

John 20:18–29

THE INCREDULITY OF THOMAS
Peter Paul Rubens
Scala/Art Resource

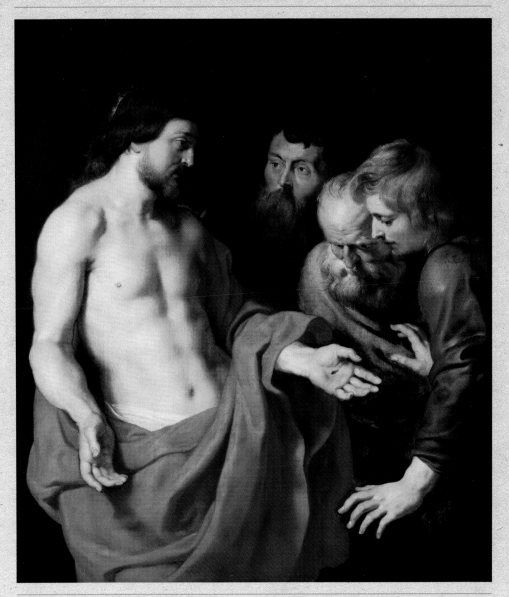

The Ascension

Until the day in which he was taken up, after that he through the Holy Ghost had given commandments unto the apostles whom he had chosen:

To whom also he shewed himself alive after his passion by many infallible proofs, being seen of them forty days, and speaking of the things pertaining to the kingdom of God:

And, being assembled together with them, commanded them that they should not depart from Jerusalem, but wait for the promise of the Father, which, saith he, ye have heard of me.

For John truly baptized with water; but ye shall be baptized with the Holy Ghost not many days hence. When they therefore were come together, they asked of him, saying, Lord, wilt thou at this time restore again the kingdom to Israel?

And he said unto them, It is not for you to know the times or the seasons, which the Father hath put in his own power. But ye shall receive power, after that the Holy Ghost is come upon you: and ye shall be witnesses unto me both in Jerusalem, and in all Judaea, and in Samaria, and unto the uttermost part of the earth.

And when he had spoken these things, while they beheld, he was taken up; and a cloud received him out of their sight.

And while they looked steadfastly toward heaven as he went up, behold, two men stood by them in white apparel; Which also said, Ye men of Galilee, why stand ye gazing up into heaven? this same Jesus, which is taken up from you into heaven, shall so come in like manner as ye have seen him go into heaven.

Acts 1:2–11

THE ASCENSION
Adriaen van der Werff
SuperStock

The Day of Pentecost

And when the day of Pentecost was fully come, they were all with one accord in one place. And suddenly there came a sound from heaven as of a rushing mighty wind, and it filled all the house where they were sitting. And there appeared unto them cloven tongues like as of fire, and it sat upon each of them.

And they were all filled with the Holy Ghost, and began to speak with other tongues, as the Spirit gave them utterance. And there were dwelling at Jerusalem Jews, devout men, out of every nation under heaven. Now when this was noised abroad, the multitude came together, and were confounded, because that every man heard them speak in his own language. And they were all amazed and marvelled, saying one to another, Behold, are not all these which speak Galilaeans? And how hear we every man in our own tongue, wherein we were born? . . .

And they were all amazed, and were in doubt, saying one to another, What meaneth this? Others mocking said, These men are full of new wine.

But Peter, standing up with the eleven, lifted up his voice, and said unto them, Ye men of Judaea, and all ye that dwell at Jerusalem, be this known unto you, and hearken to my words: For these are not drunken, as ye suppose, seeing it is but the third hour of the day.

But this is that which was spoken by the prophet Joel; And it shall come to pass in the last days, saith God, I will pour out of my Spirit upon all flesh: and your sons and your daughters shall prophesy, and your young men shall see visions, and your old men shall dream dreams. . . . And it shall come to pass, that whosoever shall call on the name of the Lord shall be saved.

Acts 2:1–8, 12–17, 21

THE DAY OF PENTECOST
Tiziano Vecelli
S. Maria della Salute, Venice, Italy
Scala/Art Resource, NY

Christians prepare

their hearts

for the Easter season

in different ways. Some preparations

are formal and based in church tradition.

Others seek only a

humble spirit as Easter week approaches.

But Christians everywhere

come to the Easter season

spiritually on their knees.

A Time of
PREPARATION

A Season of Preparation

For forty days before Easter, many Christians the world over observe a period known as Lent. This is a time for personal contemplation, reflection, and preparation of the soul in order to fully appreciate and understand the sacrifice of Jesus Christ and the gracious gift of salvation from God. The custom of fasting during this time is a physical denial that focuses the soul and mind. Just as Jesus retreated into the wilderness and fasted for forty days to prepare for his ministry, so do many Christians follow his example.

Then was Jesus led up of the Spirit into the wilderness to be tempted of the devil. And when he had fasted forty days and forty nights, he was afterward an hungred. And when the tempter came to him, he said, If thou be the Son of God, command that these stones be made bread. But he answered and said, It is written, Man shall not live by bread alone, but by every word that proceedeth out of the mouth of God.

Then the devil taketh him up into the holy city, and setteth him on a pinnacle of the temple, And saith unto him, If thou be the Son of God, cast thyself down: for it is written, He shall give his angels charge concerning thee: and in their hands they shall bear thee up, lest at any time thou dash thy foot against a stone.

Jesus said unto him, It is written again, Thou shalt not tempt the Lord thy God.

Again, the devil taketh him up into an exceeding high mountain, and sheweth him all the kingdoms of the world, and the glory of them; And saith unto him, All these things will I give thee, if thou wilt fall down and worship me.

Then saith Jesus unto him, Get thee hence, Satan: for it is written, Thou shalt worship the Lord thy God, and him only shalt thou serve.

Then the devil leaveth him, and, behold, angels came and ministered unto him.

Matthew 4:1–11

OF FEASTING AND FASTING

Hear my prayer, O LORD,

give ear to my supplica-

tions: in thy faithfulness

answer me, and in thy

righteousness. Cause me to

hear thy loving kindness

in the morning; for in

thee do I trust: cause me

to know the way wherein

I should walk; for I lift up

my soul unto thee.

Psalm 143: 1, 8

IN MANY COUNTRIES, the days leading up to the season of preparation, the period of Lent, are marked by festivities and feasting on foods that will be avoided for the next forty days. In some cases the theme is primarily that of a festive celebration, in complete opposition to the solemnity of the next forty days. In others, it is meant as a time of cleansing and preparation for the forty days of Lent. Whether the days before Lent are known as the Italian *Carnivale*, French *Carnival*, Danish *Fastelaven*, or the New Orleans Mardi Gras, there are feasts, festivities, and foods that mark these events. Carnival, from the Latin for "farewell to the flesh," and the German *Fasnacht*, "night of the fast," are celebrated around the world with feasts aplenty.

Many countries still practice centuries-old customs which take place before Lent. The most common day for these events is Shrove

Tuesday, or, as it is sometimes called, Fat Tuesday, from the French words *mardi gras*. In many instances Shrove Tuesday concludes a three-day celebration known as Shrovetide.

The old English term "shrove" comes from a word that means "to forgive." As explained in the Anglo-Saxon *Ecclesiastical Institutes* (circa A.D. 1000): "In the week immediately before Lent everyone shall go to his confessor and confess his deeds and the confessor shall so shrive him as he

then might hear by his deeds what he is to do [in the form of penance]."

In many countries, the custom of spring cleaning stems directly from preparing for the observance of Easter. First the soul is cleansed, and then the rest of the house. Old clothes are mended and new clothes are purchased at this time of year. In the Ukraine, houses are traditionally whitewashed inside and out during Lent to welcome the season of salvation and rebirth.

Easter Celebration of Lights
Oaxaca, Mexico
Hollenbeck/International Stock

The Tradition of Shrove Tuesday

nd Jesus answered them, saying, The hour is come, that the Son of man should be glorified. Verily, verily, I say unto you, Except a corn of wheat fall into the ground and die, it abideth alone: but if it die, it bringeth forth much fruit. He that loveth his life shall lose it; and he that hateth his life in this world shall keep it unto life eternal. If any man serve me, let him follow me; and where I am, there shall also my servant be: if any man serve me, him will my Father honour. Now is my soul troubled; and what shall I say? Father, save me from this hour: but for this cause came I unto this hour. Father, glorify thy name. Then came there a voice from heaven, saying, I have both glorified it, and will glorify it again.

John 12:23–28

But hark, I hear the
*   pancake bell,*
And fritters make a
*   gallant smell;*
The cooks are baking,
*   frying, boyling,*
Stewing, mincing,
*   cutting, broyling,*
Carving, gormandising,
*   roasting,*
Carbonading, cracking,
*   slashing, toasting.*
Pancakes and fritters,
*   Say the bells of*
Saint Peter's!
*   Author Unknown*

TRADITIONALLY SHROVE TUESDAY is the day on which rich food items are used up before the upcoming fasting period. Eggs and butter find their way onto many plates across Europe. In Germany there are doughnuts (*fastnachtskuchen*), pancakes (*koekebakken*), and waffles (*wafelen*); in Norway there are *fastelavnboller* buns; and in Sweden, *Fet Tisdays bullar*. In the Netherlands there is *worstebrod*, which appears to be a plain loaf of bread but is filled with sausage.

In Olney, England, the look of Shrove Tuesday is quite different. Olney is the home of a now famous Pancake Race, the origins of which are uncertain. One story relates that a woman who was making her family's pancakes did not hear the bell calling her to shriving service at church. Upon finally hearing the bells, she ran to the church, skillet in hand. Thus, she became the first pancake racer. Yet another story relates that a bell ringer for the church rang the bell early in anticipation of the holiday's festivities. The unsuspecting cook, caught off guard, raced to the church.

History tells us that Shrove Tuesday of 1445 marked the date of the first race, which was held each year until World War II, when it was discontinued until its revival in 1948.

In Olney the race is run by women who must be residents over the age of eighteen. Dressed in traditional skirts, aprons, and head coverings, they run from the Market Place to a point midway down Church Lane—a total distance of about 415 yards. Everyone gathers in the center of town to watch the racers run while holding skillets of still-cooking pancakes. They dash to the church, flipping their pancakes as they run. The winner must flip the pancakes at least three times before reaching the church.

SHROVE TUESDAY PANCAKE RACE
Olney, England
FPG International

The starter calls contestants to "Toss your pancakes. Are you ready?" The race is begun with the pancake bell—an echo of the shriving bell, which called people to church to be "shriven" or forgiven. The winner is greeted by, "The peace of the Lord be always with you" spoken by the vicar. All who finish the course attend the Shrove Tuesday service, during which prizes are presented.

In 1950, the town of Liberal, Kansas, challenged Olney to a race after seeing photos of the race at Olney and learning of its history. It is now an annual competition. The winner of the race is declared after Liberal telephones Olney to compare the race times of the English and American winners.

Fastnachtskuchen

This is a Shrove Tuesday German tradition carried on by the Pennsylvania Dutch. Shrove Tuesday morning fastnachtskuchen *are prepared to be eaten during the day. The last piece of the dough is dropped into the hot oil before breakfast, and when it is done it is presented to* die Fastnacht, *the lazy person who is the last to make it to the breakfast table.*

INGREDIENTS

3¾ to 4¼ cups all-purpose flour
⅓ cup sugar
½ teaspoon salt
1 package active dry yeast
¼ cup margarine, softened
1 cup very warm water
1 egg, room temperature
   Vegetable oil

DIRECTIONS *(makes 32)*

In a large bowl, combine 1¼ cups of the flour, sugar, salt, and dry yeast; blend well. Stir in margarine. Gradually stir in warm (120°–130° F) water. Beat 2 minutes on medium speed of electric mixer, scraping bowl occasionally. Add egg and ½ cup of the remaining flour, or enough to make a thick batter. Beat on high speed 2 minutes, scraping bowl occasionally. Stir in enough of the remaining flour to make a soft dough. Place in a greased bowl, turning once to grease top. Cover and let rise in a warm, draft-free place until doubled in bulk, about 1 hour. Punch dough down and turn out onto a lightly floured surface. Knead until smooth and elastic, about 8 to 10 minutes. Roll out dough into an 8-x-16-inch rectangle. Cut into 2-inch squares. Cut a slit about ¼-inch deep into each, without cutting completely through. Place squares on ungreased baking sheets. Cover and let rise until doubled in bulk, about 45 minutes. Heat oil in electric fryer or deep skillet to 375° F. Drop dough squares into hot oil and fry until golden brown on both sides. Drain on paper towels. Dip warm doughnuts in granulated sugar, if desired.

A COUNTRY CHURCH
Ramsau, Germany
Miwako Ikeda/International Stock

The Tradition of Ash Wednesday

When Mordecai perceived all that was done, Mordecai rent his clothes, and put on sackcloth with ashes, and went out into the midst of the city, and cried with a loud and a bitter cry; And came even before the king's gate: for none might enter into the king's gate clothed with sackcloth. And in every province, whithersoever the king's commandment and his decree came, there was great mourning among the Jews, and fasting, and weeping, and wailing; and many lay in sackcloth and ashes.

Esther 4:1–3

IN ANCIENT TIMES, people marked times of fasting, prayer, and repentance by placing ashes on their foreheads. This was considered to be an expression of the forty days of reflection and prayer that would follow.

The name *dies cinerum*, day of ashes, probably dates from at least the eighth century. In most churches, the ashes for the Ash Wednesday service come from burning the palm fronds from the previous year's Palm Sunday celebration.

According to ancient custom, in some churches the faithful are exhorted to approach the altar and receive a mark of ashes on their foreheads in the sign of the cross, as these words are spoken: "Remember, man, that thou art dust and unto dust thou shalt return."

ALTHOUGH INFREQUENTLY used now, the service of Tenebrae is still observed in a few churches today. It is a lovely ceremony that begins on Ash Wednesday and ends on Good Friday. Over the course of the three days, lit candles are gradually extinguished after selected readings are done. The service symbolizes the desertion of Christ by the twelve apostles. The service is ended when the last remaining lit candle is extinguished, representing the burial of Christ.

Before the advent of the calendar, the Lenten season was sometimes counted out by using ingenious methods of measuring time. In Greece, for example, the mechanism used to keep time was that of seven hen feathers inserted into a boiled potato or onion. The feather-ridden vegetable, called the kuharas, *was hung from the ceiling. As the weeks of Lent passed, one feather was removed each week.*

CHURCH CHOIR
SuperStock

Ash Wednesday Pretzels

The pretzel, perhaps because of its sheer simplicity, is considered a fasting food and therefore appropriate to the Lenten season. The word pretzel comes from the Latin word, pretiolum, *which means "a little prize." In the fifth century, Italian monks made pretzels and gave them to the poor as well as to good students. The shape of the pretzel, however, may have been derived from the monks who made them, showing their arms crossed in prayer. In Europe, the simple Ash Wednesday pretzel sometimes is transformed into a more elaborate and richer Easter treat when made with eggs, cheese, and butter, and even dipped in chocolate.*

INGREDIENTS

2¾ cups sifted all-purpose flour
1 package active dry yeast
1 tablespoon sugar
¼ teaspoon salt
1 cup very warm water
   (120° to 130° F)
2 tablespoons vegetable oil
2 quarts water
⅓ cup baking soda
Coarse salt

THE CHURCH OF SANTA MARIA DELLA SALUTE
Francesco Guardi
The Lowe Art Museum, University of Miami
SuperStock

DIRECTIONS *(makes 12)*

In a large mixer bowl, combine 1¼ cups of the flour, yeast, sugar, and salt; mix well. Add warm water and oil. Blend at low speed of mixer until moistened; beat 3 minutes at medium speed. By hand, gradually stir in enough remaining flour to make a firm dough. Knead on floured surface until smooth and elastic. Place in greased bowl, turning to grease top. Cover and let rise in warm place until light and doubled, about 1 hour. Punch down dough. Divide into 12 equal pieces. On lightly floured surface, roll each piece into an 18-inch rope. Shape into a circle, overlapping 4 inches from each end. Twist ends at the point where dough overlaps. Lift ends across to the opposite edge of circle; tuck under to make a pretzel shape. Place on greased cookie sheets. Let rise, uncovered, about 20 minutes. In a 3-quart non-aluminum pan, bring water and soda to a rolling boil. Lower 1 or 2 pretzels into saucepan for 10 seconds each side. Lift from water with slotted spoon or spatula; drain. Place on well-greased cookie sheets. Let dry briefly. Brush with egg white; sprinkle with coarse salt. Bake in a preheated 425° F oven for 12 to 15 minutes until browned. Remove from cookie sheet. Serve warm with butter or mustard. Best if served immediately.

The crowds thronged the street
as Jesus entered Jerusalem.
The people hailed Him
as King.
They might have thought that
He would free them
from the rule of Rome.
They had seen the Saviour.
But the struggle
was yet to come.

Palm
SUNDAY

Palm Sunday

*A*nd many spread their garments in the way: and others cut down branches off the trees, and strawed them in the way. And they that went before, and they that followed, cried, saying, Hosanna; Blessed is he that cometh in the name of the Lord: Blessed be the kingdom of our father David, that cometh in the name of the Lord: Hosanna in the highest. And Jesus entered into Jerusalem, and into the temple.

Mark 11:8–11

DURING CHRIST'S LIFETIME, it was the custom for the common people throughout the Roman Empire to greet royalty by waving palm branches and strewing them in the path of the royal personages. The palm itself was symbolic of victory; Roman generals and their armies often carried palms in triumphal processions returning from battle. So it was when Jesus entered Jerusalem on what we now call Palm Sunday.

Palm Sunday marks the beginning of Holy Week—the observation of the last week of Christ's life, which leads up to His death and Resurrection. All over the world, Christians use palm branches in church services and joyous processions and parades. Where palms are unavailable, other plants are used, but the meaning is still the same. This was Jesus' triumphant entry, the procession of a King, the conqueror of evil. But the procession, although joyous, also marked the beginning of the last week of Christ's life on earth.

Carol of the Children

Our Lord came to Jerusalem
  On that first Palm Sunday,
Not clad in royal robe of fur,
  Nor festive garment gay.
No steed had He to ride upon,
  No kingly palfrey,
But meekly on a lowly beast,
  Rode slowly on His way.

And as He drew near to the gates,
  The people thronged around,
They cut palm branches from the trees
  And spread them on the ground,
The little children flocked to Him,
  And sweetly they did sing
Hosanna, Hosanna,
  Hosanna to the King.

Author Unknown

AT THE ENTRANCE TO THE TEMPLE MOUNT, JERUSALEM
Gustav Bauernfeind
Christie's Images/SuperStock

Palm Sunday in the Holy Land

O Jerusalem, Jerusalem, thou that killest the prophets, and stonest them which are sent unto thee, how often would I have gathered thy children together, even as a hen gathereth her chickens under her wings, and ye would not! Behold, your house is left unto you desolate. For I say unto you, Ye shall not see me henceforth, till ye shall say, Blessed is he that cometh in the name of the Lord. And Jesus went out, and departed from the temple: and his disciples came to him for to shew him the buildings of the temple. And Jesus said unto them, See ye not all these things? verily I say unto you, There shall not be left here one stone upon another, that shall not be thrown down.

Matthew 23:37–39; 24:1–2

The Ride to Jerusalem

The colt is tethered at the
    appointed gate,
The password known: "The
    Lord hath need of him";
The trees are ready—this
    year Easter's late—
And willows wave their
    feather-fronds of palm.

The starlings practise on the
    chimney pots;
The thoroughfares of time
    are open wide;
Soon, now, the eyes shall weep
    for the blind streets,
The healing voice shall speak
    to the deaf road.

FOR CENTURIES Christian pilgrims have traveled to the Holy Land to see and worship at the places they have read about in the Gospels. The most popular time for these pilgrimages is the week before Easter, and the most popular city is Jerusalem. Visitors are able to witness the reenactment of the events that led up to Christ's Resurrection, from His triumphant entry into the city on Palm Sunday to His death and burial.

Palm Sunday, the day when Jesus entered Jerusalem, marks the beginning of the holiest week in the Christian calendar. Jesus almost certainly took the Hosanna Road down the Mount of Olives after spending the night in Bethany. His footsteps are retraced every year by a joyful procession of pilgrims, schoolchildren, and teachers led by the Latin patriarch. The steep, rocky road comes alive as the pilgrims sing songs of praise and wave palm branches. All along the way they can view the city of Jerusalem, its narrow streets and golden buildings looking much as they must have when Jesus surveyed them and mourned over the coming destruction of the city: "O Jerusalem, Jerusalem, thou that killest

the prophets and stonest them which are sent unto thee, how often would I have gathered thy children together, even as a hen gathereth her chickens under her wings, and ye would not!" (Matthew 23:37).

The only gate visible from the Mount of Olives is the Golden Gate, which marks the spot where Jesus entered the city. The actual gate through which He passed was the old Zusan Gate, which was destroyed by the Romans in A.D. 70. Since the ninth century, the Golden Gate has been walled up by the Moslems, who fear that it might provide entry for an invader more intent on earthly conquest than was the King who entered on that Palm Sunday almost 2,000 years ago.

The window-sills are empty;
  no crowds wait;
Here at the pavement's edge
  I watch alone.
Master, like sunlight strike
  my slaty heart
And ask not acclamations
  from the stone.

Norman Nicholson

Jerusalem from the Mount of Olives
Gustav Bauernfeind
Christie's Images/SuperStock

The Holy City

Words by F. E. Weatherly • Music by Stephen Adams

Last night I lay a-sleep-ing, there came a dream so fair; I stood in old Je-ru-sa-lem be-side the tem-ple there. I heard the chil-dren sing-ing, and ev-er as they sang, me thought the voice of an-gels from heav'n in an-swer rang; Me thought the voice of an - gels from heav'n in an - swer rang, Je - ru - sa - lem! Je - ru - sa - lem! Lift up your

The Holy City

The Holy City

The Holy City

pass a - way! Je - ru - sa - lem! Je - ru - sa -
lem! Sing for the night is o'er! Ho - san -
na in the high - est! Ho - san - na for - ev - er - more!
Ho - san - na in the high - est! Ho -
san - na for - ev - er - more!

PALM SUNDAY AROUND THE WORLD

THE DONKEY

When fishes flew
   and forests walked
And figs grew upon thorn,
Some moment when
   the moon was blood
Then surely I was born.
With monstrous head
   and sickening cry
And ears like errant wings,
The devil's walking parody
On all four-footed things.

FINLAND In parts of the country, Palm Sunday is called Willowswitch Sunday, and the day before Palm Sunday is referred to as Willowswitch Saturday. It is the custom for children to cut willow switches early on Saturday and decorate them with colorful cloth streamers. The children go from door to door with their willow switches, looking for the lady of the house. Upon finding her, the children lightly strike her with their switches and sing, "Switching, switching, switches go, wishing freshness and health for the year." In exchange for the well-wishes of the children, the lucky lady of the family returns wishes for good health.

GREECE With beautiful artistry, the people of Greece weave palm fronds into intricate shapes in honor of Palm Sunday. The shapes include stars, baskets, and crosses. Where palm branches are readily available, churches are decorated both inside and out. In northern provinces, myrtle and bay are substituted for palms. Each family keeps these symbolic woven pieces of art as reminders in the frame of one of the house's religious paintings.

SPAIN Probably nowhere else in the world pays the homage to Holy Week that Spain does. Although many places in Europe have special events for this week, Spain is noted for literally thousands of processions, ranging in location from small villages to the larger cities. In Seville alone, a procession is held every day of the week until Easter.

CZECHOSLOVAKIA Farmers believe that waving blessed pussy willows over their fields will prevent violent damage to their crops. On Palm Sunday, children search the woods for pussy willows. They collect branches, especially those which have not sprouted, and decorate them with small paper flowers and bright feathers for use on Easter Day.

MEXICO Called *Domingo de las Palmas,* Palm Sunday is a great occasion for the people of Mexico, who carry large bouquets of flowers, palms, and laurel to the church and then on to their homes. Many Mexicans believe that if the flowers are kept through the years, they will help protect against illness.

NETHERLANDS On Palm Sunday, children walk the country-side carrying a *palmpass* (the Easter palm). The *palmpass* is a hoop attached to a stick and decorated with a variety of Easter symbols. Decorations range from oranges, figs, and even small cakes, to egg shells and paper flags. Competitions are held in some places to recognize and award the *palmpass* which shows all the correct symbols and is the most unique. As the children walk, each with his or her *palmpass,* they sing:

> One more Sunday
> And we'll get an egg,
> And we'll get an egg.
> One egg is no egg;
> Two eggs are half an egg;
> Three eggs are an Easter egg!

POLAND The palms used in Poland on Palm Sunday are really pussy willows. They are put in water so that they will bloom by Easter Sunday, which is called Flowering Sunday. Here, as is true in many European countries, the people believe in the curative powers of flowers related to Easter. Many Poles believe that swallowing a catkin from a pussy willow will protect against a sore throat.

WALES The Welsh celebrate Palm Sunday in a way similar to the American observance of Memorial Day. On Palm Sunday, the Welsh take flowers to the graves of their loved ones. Hence, they refer to this day as Flowering Sunday.

The tattered outlaw
of the earth,
Of ancient crooked will;
Starve, scourge, deride
me: I am dumb,
I keep my secret still.
Fools! For I also had
my hour;
One far fierce hour
and sweet:
There was a shout
about my ears,
And palms before my feet.

G. K. Chesterton

On Thursday, Jesus went
  with His disciples
  to eat the Passover.
    In that room, it was a time
of fellowship, of quiet reflection,
of betrayal, and of commitment.
    Over and over,
Jesus showed His love:
in the washing of the feet,
in the prayer in Gethsemane,
and finally, in submission.

The
LAST SUPPER

THE CHURCH OF
GETHSEMANE
Jerusalem, Israel
R. Kord/H. Armstrong Roberts

ANCIENT OLIVE TREES IN THE
GARDEN OF GETHSEMANE
Jerusalem, Israel
R. Kord/H. Armstrong Roberts

Maundy Thursday in Jerusalem

ow is the judgment of this world: now shall the prince of this world be cast out. And I, if I be lifted up from the earth, will draw all men unto me. This he said, signifying what death he should die. The people answered him, We have heard out of the law that Christ abideth for ever: and how sayest thou, The Son of man must be lifted up? who is this Son of man? Then Jesus said unto them, Yet a little while is the light with you. Walk while ye have the light, lest darkness come upon you: for he that walketh in darkness knoweth not whither he goeth. While ye have light, believe in the light, that ye may be the children of light. These things spake Jesus, and departed, and did hide himself from them. But though he had done so many miracles before them, yet they believed not on him.

John 12:31–37

THE DAYS BETWEEN Palm Sunday and Maundy Thursday were marked in Christ's life not by outstanding events of triumph or suffering but by the teachings and miracles that characterized His ministry. For this reason, in most churches, there are no services after Palm Sunday until Maundy Thursday.

On Thursday, Jesus and His disciples gathered in an upper room of a building in Jerusalem to eat the Passover. Here Jesus washed the disciples' feet, shared bread and wine with them, and foretold His betrayal by Judas. Then He went to the Garden of Gethsemane with His disciples, where He prayed and then was betrayed by Judas and arrested. Late that night, Jesus' unofficial trial took place before Jewish authorities.

Many of the events of Maundy Thursday are commemorated in dignified services held by different religious groups in Jerusalem. On Thursday night, many Christians go to the Garden of Gethsemane on the Mount of Olives. Even during Holy Week today, a sense of peace pervades this small garden outside the city. The only voices heard are raised in prayer. The olive trees are ancient. Some of them are old enough to have witnessed the Lord's agony.

Maundy Thursday

*I*f God be glorified in him, God shall also glorify him in himself, and shall straightway glorify him. Little children, yet a little while I am with you. Ye shall seek me: and as I said unto the Jews, Whither I go, ye cannot come; so now I say to you. A new commandment I give unto you, That ye love one another; as I have loved you, that ye also love one another. By this shall all men know that ye are my disciples, if ye have love one to another.

John 13:32–35

THE THURSDAY BEFORE EASTER is sometimes called Maundy Thursday. There are several interpretations of the derivation of the word *maundy,* one linking it to the old French word *maundier* which means "to beg." Another version of the story gives it a Saxon meaning, claiming it is derived from the word *maund,* meaning a hamper used to store food. Traditionally, Maundy Thursday was a day for giving food to the poor.

More likely, the derivation is that of a Latin word, *maund,* which means "to command." Thursday was the evening of the Lord's Supper, during which Christ said to His disciples: "A new commandment I give unto you, That ye love one another; as I have loved you, that ye also love one another."

Several traditions are associated with Maundy Thursday. Bells have a great significance on this day. They are rung loudly during the church service and then remain silent until Easter Sunday. The ancient ceremony of foot washing is still practiced in some churches on Maundy Thursday. During the time of Christ, people wore sandals, which were unable to keep out the dust. Because it was poor manners to enter a house wearing shoes, servants would wash the feet of guests upon their arrival. After the meal of the Last Supper, Christ showed His followers in word and deed the ultimate respect He had for them and the respect He wished them to carry on in His memory: He gently washed their feet. Where the ceremony is practiced today, during the Maundy Thursday service, twelve members of the congregation who have been chosen to represent the apostles have their right foot washed by a high-ranking clergyman or deacon. Music fills the air as the ceremony is humbly and dutifully performed.

BELL OF THE CHURCH OF OUR LADY PROSIANI
Naxos, Greek Islands
Ellen Rooney/International Stock

A Legacy of Faith through Art

FOR MOST OF US, when we think of the Last Supper, we visualize the great painting by that name, the masterpiece of Leonardo da Vinci. So it has been throughout the centuries. The greatness of Leonardo's mural was recognized as soon as he finished painting it on the refectory wall in the Church of Santa Maria delle Grazie in Milan. Onlookers watched him scramble up the scaffolding to work from dawn until sundown, without stopping to eat or drink. Then for days he would not touch the painting but spent several hours examining and critiquing it.

Unfortunately, almost as soon as it was completed, the painting began to decay, due in part to the medium the artist used to accommodate his thoughtful, hesitant method of working. Da Vinci could not use the fresco technique popular at the time because it dried too quickly to allow changes. So he devised a technique of his own. He coated the wall with a ground mixture of gesso, pitch, and mastic, which he expected would absorb the tempera-emulsion paint as well as protect the paint against moisture.

The passage of time demonstrated that the ground coat was not one of da Vinci's successful inventions. Soon the pigment began to flake from the wall. Reports from as early as 1517 note that the painting was beginning to decay, a process which has continued into our own century. And as if the painting's tendency to self-destruct were not enough, man aided in its destruction. In 1652 a door was cut into the wall that damaged the lower central portion of the painting.

In 1726, the task of restoration was undertaken by the painter Michelangelo Bellotti. In a mistaken belief that the painting was oil-based, Bellotti gave the whole mural a coat of oil varnish. Thus began a long series of attempted restorations which may have done more harm than good to the painting.

In 1770, Guiseppe Mazza, also a painter, attempted to repair the work of Bellotti by removing the retouching with a paint scraper. Fortunately, his efforts, when discovered, were stopped. But Mazza had already scraped over all the figures of the painting except three apostles. A more

During the Second World War, a bomb fell on the Church of Santa Maria delle Grazie, almost completely destroying it. Miraculously, the wall with the painting of The Last Supper *remained standing. A metal frame with a protective shield placed before it acted as a support and saved the painting.*

constructive attempt at preserving the painting was made in 1789. This was not a restoration but a reconstruction of what the painting must have looked like when new, based on a close study of the original. The result, by André Dutertre on behalf of Louis XVI of France, is one of the best copies of this masterpiece ever produced.

In 1819, Stefano Barezzi claimed that he could remove the painting from the wall. His technique had been successful in removing several frescoes from other churches. The authorities insisted that he test his method on a small portion of the painting. Unfortunately, he tested on a portion of Christ's hand. The result was a disaster, and Barezzi was ordered to stop. Years later, he again applied for permission to restore the painting, this time not by removing it but by anchoring the flecks of paint with glue. This attempt proved to be more successful.

Despite all efforts to save the painting, it seemed headed for gradual deterioration and eventual destruction. Over the years attempts were made to restore the original environmental conditions to the refectory. Windows were opened to provide natural lighting. Other efforts were designed to control the humidity in the room and the moisture of the wall on which *The Last Supper* was painted. The result was that the paint flaked off, and the painting developed mold.

With reconstruction after the damage done to the church by World War II, officials employed the latest methods of conservation on the painting as well as on the wall itself. That restoration was completed in 1954. It involved gluing thousands of particles of paint to the wall by means of a shellac solution. During the restoration, much of the original paint surface was rediscovered. While there were high hopes that this would be the final restoration necessary to preserve *The Last Supper,* the process of deterioration still continues. New attempts at restoration are ongoing. Still, when considering the amazing history of its 500 years, it is miraculous that the painting has survived so long.

Leonardo da Vinci was born in 1452 and died in 1519. He was the son of a Florentine notary. At the age of forty-three, he began The Last Supper. *He completed it in three years.*

Leonardo da Vinci, in addition to being a painter, was a sculptor, architect, engineer, and scientist. He left many notebooks containing his notes on research into the fields of anatomy, architecture, hydraulics, hydrology, geology, meteorology, mechanics, machinery and gears, military weaponry and fortifications, human and avian flight, optics, mathematics, and botany.

In the Garden

Words and music by C. Austin Miles

1. I come to the gar-den a - lone, While the dew is still on the
2. He speaks, and the sound of His voice Is so sweet the birds hush their
3. I'd stay in the gar-den with Him Tho the night a - round me be

ros - es; And the voice I hear, fall - ing on my ear, The Son of God dis -
sing-ing; And the mel - o - dy that He gave to me With - in my heart is
fall - ing; But He bids me go; thro' the voice of woe, His voice to me is

clos - es.
ring - ing. And He walks with me, and He talks with me, And He tells me I am His
call - ing.

own, And the joy we share as we tar - ry there, None oth - er has ev - er known.

A VIEW OF JERUSALEM
Mrs. Robertson Blaine
Christie's Images/SuperStock

'Tis Midnight

'Tis midnight; and on Olive's brow
The star is dimmed that lately shone:
'Tis midnight; in the garden now
The suffering Saviour prays alone.

'Tis midnight; and from all removed,
The Saviour wrestles lone with fears;
E'en that disciple whom He loved
Heeds not his Master's grief and tears.

'Tis midnight; and from heavenly plains
Is borne the song that angels know;
Unheard by mortals are the strains
That sweetly soothe the Saviour's woe.
William B. Tappan

In Gethsemane

Sweet Eden was the arbor of delight,
Yet in its honey flowers our poison blew:
Sad Gethsemane, the bower of baleful night,
Where Christ a health of poison for us drew,
Yet all our honey in that poison grew:
So we, from sweetest flower, could suck our bane,
And Christ, from bitter venom, could again
Extract life out of death, and pleasure out of pain.
Giles Fletcher

Maundy Thursday Around the World

Pange Lingua

Of the glorious Body telling,

O my tongue, its mysteries sing,

And the Blood, all price excelling,

Which the world's eternal King,

In a noble womb once dwelling,

Shed for this world's ransoming.

At the last great Supper lying

Circled by His bretheren's band,

Meekly with the law complying,

First He finished its command,

Then, immortal Food supplying,

Gave Himself with His own hand.

FRANCE In the province of Alsace, the benches and chairs of the churches are beaten with small wooden hammers. Sometimes even the exterior of the church is included in this custom. In other areas of the country, this custom occurs on Good Friday as a call to church services and replaces the ringing of the bells.

MACEDONIA, GREECE Around the year 1900, the people of Macedonia began hanging red handkerchiefs from balconies and windows on Maundy Thursday. Easter eggs are dyed red on this day, and the mother takes the first colored egg and passes it across her child's face and neck, saying, "May you grow as red as this egg and as strong as a stone." Many women also bake turtledove cakes, which are shaped like birds and have cloves for eyes.

THE UKRAINE Here, Maundy Thursday is called "Thursday of the Passion." On this day Ukrainians traditionally bathe in a river, since river water is believed by some to have special healing powers on this day.

ENGLAND At one time, Maundy Thursday, also called Royal Maundy, was the customary day for the English king and queen to wash the feet of a number of poor subjects; the number of subjects washed was the same as the number of years in the king and queen's ages. The custom was replaced by giving "Maundy Money" to the poor. The practice has changed slightly over the years but remains a tradition today in the form of specially minted coins given to selected recipients.

FINLAND The Finns believe that good weather on Maundy Thursday, which is also called Tail Thursday, will ensure good weather for the following forty days. It is customary to trim the cow's tail on this day.

SWITZERLAND Historical processions are held on what is called Green Thursday in some parts of the country. The beautiful and artistic presentation of the procession represents Christ's journey to Golgotha. The actor portraying Christ is accompanied by additional actors, dressed in full costume, portraying Roman soldiers, knights, and biblical personalities.

SWEDEN Maundy Thursday is known as Sheer Thursday, from a Swedish word meaning clean. It is also called *Kiira* ("evil spirit") Thursday. According to tradition, Easter hags, or witches, fly on their brooms to frolic with the devil on this day. People traditionally build bonfires, shoot guns, paint crosses over their doors, and hang crossed scythes in their stables to protect themselves against these witches. A more modern custom, the sending of "Easter letters," is widespread in western Sweden. The letters are secretly placed under doors and in mailboxes; the identity of the sender is not disclosed.

ITALY Sometimes referred to as the Day of the Green Ones, those seeking readmission to the church would wear bits of green herbs on this day. This custom dates to the time when Catholic penitents did this after they carried out a prescribed penance during Lent and were close to their day of readmission.

Therefore we, before Him bending,
This great Sacrament revere;
Types and shadows have their
  ending,
For the newer rite is here;
Faith, our outward sense
  befriending,
Makes the inward vision clear.

Glory let us give, and blessing
To the Father, and the Son;
Honour, might, and praise
  addressing,
While eternal ages run;
Ever too His love confessing,
Who, from both, with both is One.
Amen.

  Thomas Aquinas

The Holy Grail

A nd when the hour was come, he sat down, and the twelve apostles with him. And he said unto them, With desire I have desired to eat this passover with you before I suffer: For I say unto you, I will not any more eat thereof, until it be fulfilled in the kingdom of God. And he took the cup, and gave thanks, and said, Take this, and divide it among yourselves: For I say unto you, I will not drink of the fruit of the vine, until the kingdom of God shall come. And he took bread, and gave thanks, and brake it, and gave unto them, saying, This is my body which is given for you: this do in remembrance of me. Likewise also the cup after supper, saying, This cup is the new testament in my blood, which is shed for you.

Luke 22:14–20

THE LEGEND OF THE HOLY GRAIL is one of the most enduring in Western European literature and art. The Holy Grail is said to be the cup used at the Last Supper. It is also known as the Holy Chalice, the Cauldron, and the Cup of the Last Supper.

ANTIQUE GOBLET
Stift Kremsmunster, a Benedictine Abbey, Austria
SuperStock

One legend has it that the Grail was brought to Great Britain by Joseph of Arimathea, who was present at the Crucifixion. For centuries it lay hidden. It was believed that the Grail was kept in a mysterious castle in a vast wasteland guarded by the Fisher King, who suffered from a wound that would not heal. The Fisher King's recovery and the renewal of the desolate lands were dependent on finding the Holy Grail.

The Holy Grail first appears in written text in an old French verse romance, "Story of the Grail," which was written about the year 1180. Many other literary works about the Holy Grail have been written, the most well-known being Sir Thomas Malory's *Morte d'Arthur*, which he penned in the fifteenth century. The Grail appears again as a popular literary theme in the nineteenth century, in the works of Sir Walter Scott and Alfred, Lord Tennyson.

Gethsemane

In golden youth when seems the earth,
A summer-land of singing mirth,
When souls are glad and hearts are light,
And not a shadow lurks in sight,
We do not know it, but there lies,
Somewhere veiled under evening skies,
A garden which we all must see—
The Garden of Gethsemane.

With joyous steps we go our ways,
Love lends a halo to our days;
Light sorrows sail like clouds afar,
We laugh and say how glad we are.
We hurry on; and hurrying, go
Close to the border-land of woe,
That waits for you, and waits for me
Forever waits Gethsemane.

Down shadowy lanes, across strange streams,
Bridged over by our broken dreams;
Behind the misty caps of years,
Beyond the great salt fount of tears,
The garden lies. Strive as you may,
You cannot miss it in your way.
All paths that have been, or shall be,
Pass somewhere through Gethsemane.

All those who journey, soon or late,
Must pass within the garden's gate;
Must kneel alone in darkness there,
And battle with some fierce despair.
God pity those who cannot say:
"Not mine but thine"; who only pray:
"Let this cup pass," and cannot see
The purpose in Gethsemane.

     Ella Wheeler Wilcox

An Olive Tree Speaks

That night in cool Gethsemane
Christ taught us immortality.
We heard Him pray beneath our boughs
And felt His wrestling spirit's vows
While high upon her ancient hills,
Jerusalem walled in smugness slept
Nor guessed that her own Saviour wept
Beyond the Kidron's full spring rills.
We trembled with His lonely woes,
We longed to crash on all His foes,
We saw His face when He arose—
  a Conqueror!
So for His sake we cannot die,
But from our gnarled, decrepit root
Send up a new young slender shoot
To tell His victory to the sky.
Before our old self bows to earth,
We give a scion olive birth
To witness what we learned that night
When Christ slew death within our sight
And to our hushed Gethsemane
Entrusted immortality.

   Madeleine Sweeny Miller

In Valencia, Spain, what is considered to be the Holy Grail is kept at the Cathedral. The goblet is elaborately decorated with gold, agate, pearls, rubies, and emeralds. It has been in Valencia for over five hundred years and according to tradition came from a visit made by Mary, the mother of Jesus, to the Apostle James.

This was the darkest day.

Many of Jesus' friends fled

in fear and terror.

There was the pain of the Crucifixion.

There was the sorrow of the burial.

The world itself

revolted in writhing

and darkness.

Good
FRIDAY

Good Friday

And it was about the sixth hour, and there was a darkness over all the earth until the ninth hour. And the sun was darkened, and the veil of the temple was rent in the midst. And when Jesus had cried with a loud voice, he said, Father, into thy hands I commend my spirit: and having said thus, he gave up the ghost.

Luke 23:44–46

THE NAME GOOD FRIDAY is probably a corruption of the words "God's Friday" and commemorates the day Christ died upon the cross. This day is without doubt the most solemn day of the year for Christians.

Because the Bible makes reference to the sky becoming dark from noon until three o'clock in the afternoon, many church services are held during these hours to commemorate Christ's death. In many churches the altars are stripped of all linens and crosses and statuary are covered with a cloth of mourning black.

Perhaps because of the deeply solemn nature of this day, people historically were more inclined to follow superstitions on Good Friday. Housewives would not wash clothes on Good Friday because of the connection to Christ being wrapped in linen on this day. Miners were fearful of going underground this day, believing that the earth was cursed on the day Jesus was laid in His tomb. No blacksmith would pound a nail because nails were used to crucify Christ. Whereas many Christian cultures celebrate the days of Lent and Holy Week in various fashions, one thing is common to all: Good Friday is held in the utmost reverence and respect.

A Ballad of Trees and the Master

Into the woods my Master went,
 Clean forspent, forspent;
Into the woods my Master came,
 Forspent with love and shame.
But the olives they were not blind to Him,
 The little gray leaves were kind to Him,
The thorn-tree had a mind to Him,
 When into the woods He came.

Out of the woods my Master went,
 And He was well content;
Out of the woods my Master came,
 Content with death and shame.
When death and shame would woo Him last,
 From under the trees they drew Him last,
'Twas on a tree they slew Him last,
 When out of the woods He came.

Sidney Lanier

CHAPELLE DU CALVAIRE
Charles-Marie Bouton
Musée des Beaux-Arts, Rouen, France
SuperStock

Song of the Spirit

The children of Africa readily adopted the Hebrew Exodus story as their own with such songs as "When Israel was in Egypt's land / Let my people go, / Oppressed so hard they could not stand, / Let my people go."

The Crown of Roses

When Jesus Christ was yet a child
He had a garden small and wild,
Wherein He cherished roses fair
And wove them into garlands there.

Now once, as summer-time drew nigh,
There came a group of children by,
And seeing roses on the tree,
With shouts they plucked them merrily.

"Do You bind roses in Your hair?"
They cried, in scorn, to Jesus there.
The Boy said humbly: "Take, I pray,
All but the naked thorns away."

Then of the thorns they made a crown,
And with rough fingers pressed it down
Till on His forehead fair and young
Red drops of blood like roses sprung.
Peter Ilyich Tchaikovsky

WE ARE INDEBTED to the African Americans of the pre-Civil War South for some of the most beautiful, touching, and inspiring songs—Negro Spirituals—which someone has beautifully termed "Songs of the Spirit."

The spirituals were first played upon heartstrings taut with the oppression of slavery, and the Crucifixion of Jesus struck a responsive chord in the hearts of slaves. They identified with the sufferings of their Lord, who had felt the injustice and oppression of inhuman treatment. With their taskmasters whipping them into submission, the slaves could identify with the One crucified on a felon's cross. The slaves would sing with intense pathos, "Nobody knows the trouble I've seen."

The tragedy of Calvary is dramatically portrayed in "Were You There When They Crucified My Lord?" The unknown composer goes beyond the horror of Calvary to the triumph of our Lord over the cross and death. His question-and-answer format makes the words all the more poignantly personal.

The unnamed composers of these poignant and powerful spirituals had a faith that saw God's ultimate triumph beyond earth's tragedies and injustice. "Were You There When They Crucified My Lord?" is a song that enables us to see beyond the cross to the crown, beyond Good Friday to Easter Sunday, and beyond the blackest night to the glorious dawn.

Henry Gariepy

Were You There When They Crucified My Lord?

Traditional Negro Spiritual

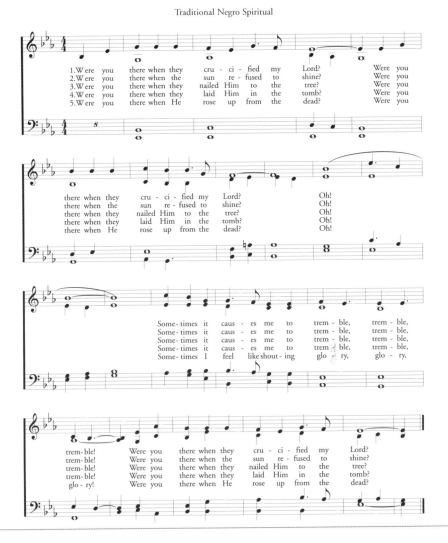

1. Were you there when they cru-ci-fied my Lord? Were you
2. Were you there when the sun re-fused to shine? Were you
3. Were you there when they nailed Him to the tree? Were you
4. Were you there when they laid Him in the tomb? Were you
5. Were you there when He rose up from the dead? Were you

there when they cru-ci-fied my Lord? Oh!
there when the sun re-fused to shine? Oh!
there when they nailed Him to the tree? Oh!
there when they laid Him in the tomb? Oh!
there when He rose up from the dead? Oh!

Some-times it caus-es me to trem-ble, trem-ble,
Some-times it caus-es me to trem-ble, trem-ble,
Some-times it caus-es me to trem-ble, trem-ble,
Some-times it caus-es me to trem-ble, trem-ble,
Some-times I feel like shout-ing glo-ry, glo-ry,

trem-ble! Were you there when they cru-ci-fied my Lord?
trem-ble! Were you there when the sun re-fused to shine?
trem-ble! Were you there when they nailed Him to the tree?
trem-ble! Were you there when they laid Him in the tomb?
glo-ry! Were you there when He rose up from the dead?

The Passion Play

*Stedefast crosse, among
   all other
Thou art a tree mickle
   of price;
In branch and flower
   wilk another
I ne wot none in
   wood no rys,
Sweete be the nailes
   and sweete be the tree,
And sweeter be the burden
   that hanges upon thee.*
       Geoffrey Chaucer

OBERAMMERGAU PASSION PLAY
*Oberammergau, Germany
Josef Beck/FPG International*

MOST OFTEN, passion plays refer to those plays that depict the suffering, Crucifixion, and Resurrection of Jesus Christ. In the Middle Ages, passion plays dedicated to the story of Christ's death and Resurrection were often staged by Europeans in small towns and villages. In these renditions, the townspeople were able to personally participate in the events of the last days of Christ's life.

Today, several towns in southern Germany, Western Austria, and Switzerland continue the tradition of the passion play, and there are over forty presentations of the passion play each year in the United States. Although passion plays are presented worldwide, the most noted of these is the passion play presented by the Bavarian village of Oberammergau. This picturesque village, rimmed by dark woodlands and snow-capped mountains, is a tight maze of cobbled streets and houses adorned with historic murals. In the summer, beautiful dairy farmsteads and immaculate fields paint the landscape. During the winter, the thousand-year-old tradition of woodcarving fills the villagers' days. Quaint Old-World shops are filled with religious statues and other wood carvings.

The Oberammergau Passion Play began in 1634 when the townspeople staged it as a thanksgiving to God for sparing their town from the plague sweeping throughout Europe. The original play was written by a monk and the music by a schoolmaster. The play, which takes over five hours to perform, is presented only once every ten years; and over 800 local performers make up the cast. Even today local residents take their original promise to honor and celebrate the life and Passion of Jesus Christ by growing their hair and beards to prepare for their latest roles.

. . . and when, throughout the world, faith falters,
When nation wars against nation,
Laying waste the earth in piteous ruin;
And into the ultimate refuge of peace
The burning brand of war is thrown—
Then will our Saviour plant, as a tree,
This play in Oberammergau
That it may beckon the sons of man
Wandering lost in dreary wastes,

Beckon them to stop awhile
And rest beneath its blessed shade
To hear the tale and learn the Way,
The tale of better need and death
Of Jesus Christ, our Lord.

     Leo Eeismentel

MURAL, HEINSELLER HOUSE
Oberammergau, Germany
M. Thonig/H. Armstrong Roberts

Golgotha

THE HILL ON WHICH CHRIST WAS CRUCIFIED is called Golgotha. Today, the hill thought to be the actual hill in Jerusalem is well marked. Pilgrims to Jerusalem walk along the Via Dolorosa, or Way of Sorrows, the street down which Christ walked from Pilate's tribunal to Calvary. Some begin their walk at the Convent of the Sisters of Zion, which is thought to be the site of Pilate's palace and tribunal. Pilgrims retrace the steps of Jesus from this spot to the Holy Sepulchre. The Church of the Holy Sepulchre is thought to be the site of Jesus' entombment and Resurrection.

Good Friday

Am I a stone and not a sheep
That I can stand, O Christ, beneath Thy Cross,
To number drop by drop Thy Blood's slow loss,
And yet not weep?

Not so those women loved
Who with exceeding grief lamented Thee;
Not so fallen Peter weeping bitterly;
Not so the thief was moved;

Not so the Sun and Moon
Which hid their faces in a starless sky,
A horror of great darkness at broad noon,
I, only I.

Yet give not o'er,
But seek Thy sheep, true Shepherd of the flock;
Greater than Moses, turn and look once more
And smite a rock.

Christina Rossetti

His Saviour's Words, Going to the Cross

Have, have ye no regard, all ye
Who pass this way, to pity me
Who am a man of misery?

A man both bruis'd, and broke, and one
Who suffers not here for mine own
But for my friends' transgression?

Ah! Sion's Daughters, do not fear
The Cross, the Cords, the Nails, the Spear,
The Myrrh, the Gall, the Vinegar;

For Christ, your loving Saviour, hath
Drunk up the wine of God's fierce wrath;
Only, there's left a little froth,

Less for to taste, than for to shew
What bitter cups had been your due,
Had He not drank them up for you.

Robert Herrick

VIA DOLOROSA
Jerusalem, Israel
Stockman/International Stock

The Merchants' Carol

As we rode down the steep hillside,
　Twelve merchants with our fairing,
A shout across the hollow land
　Came loud upon our hearing,
A shout, a song, a thousand strong,
　A thousand lusty voices:
"Make haste," said I, I knew not why,
　"Jerusalem rejoices!"

Beneath the olives fast we rode,
　And louder came the shouting:
"So great a noise must mean," said we,
　"A king, beyond all doubting!"
Spurred on, did we, this king to see,
　And left the mules to follow;
And nearer, clearer rang the noise
　Along the Kidron hollow.

Behold, a many-coloured crowd
　About the gate we found there;
But One among them all, we marked,
　One Man who made no sound there;
Still louder ever rose the crowd's
　"Hosanna in the highest!"
"O King" thought I, I know not why
　"In all this joy Thou sighest."

A Merchant:
Then He looked up, He looked at me;
　But whether He spoke I doubted:
How could I hear so calm a speech
　While all the rabble shouted?
And yet these words, it seems, I heard:
　"I shall be crowned to-morrow."
They struck my heart with sudden smart,
　And filled my bones with sorrow.

We followed far, we traded not,
　But long we could not find Him.
The very folk that called Him King
　Let robbers go and bind Him.
We found Him then, the sport of men,
　Still calm among their crying;
And well we knew His words were true—
　He was most kingly dying.
　　　　　Frank Kendon

LEFT: *THE TRADITIONAL SITE*
OF CHRIST'S TOMB
Jerusalem, Israel
R. Opfer/H. Armstrong Roberts

ABOVE: *THE HILL BELIEVED*
TO BE GOLGOTHA
Near Jerusalem, Israel
R. Opfer/H. Armstrong Roberts

GOOD FRIDAY AROUND THE WORLD

Again maternal

   Autumn grieves,

As blood-like drip

   the maple leaves

On Nature's Calvary.

And every

   sap-forsaken limb

Renews the mystery

   of Him

Who died upon a Tree.

   John Banister Tabb

NORWAY Here Good Friday is called Long Friday. One custom popular on this day can be traced back to Norse mythology. Today in many parts of northwestern Europe, branches of mountain ash are gathered and placed on the doorposts to protect against evil. The mountain ash is considered a sacred tree and therefore is thought to have great powers against witches and illness.

SWEDEN As in Norway, Good Friday is called Long Friday and is considered a solemn holiday in this country. Shops are closed, and black clothing is worn by many adults. It is traditionally forbidden to touch steel—even a needle or scissors—since it would violate the memory of Christ's suffering on this day. In older times, socializing was not done, nor were children allowed to play outdoors. To commemorate Christ's scourging, parents might use twigs of dwarf birch to give a child a light slap as a reminder of the significance of the day.

PORTUGAL As the season of Lent comes to a close, the people of Lisbon make a traditional journey to the seashore, where they gather clams to make soup.

IRELAND Good Friday in Ireland is by tradition a time of strict fasting. Very little food is eaten, and even the traditional Friday fish is replaced by small shellfish in seaside communities. Years ago, people walked barefoot to church for Good Friday services.

GERMANY In some parts of Germany, the fast of the day allows only simple *spaetzle*, or dumplings, to be served with stewed fruits for dinner. There are several superstitions associated with Good Friday: seeds sown on this day will thrive, cooled water from a hot iron will cure warts, and if it rains on this day, the whole year will be blessed.

ETHIOPIA Good Friday begins a fast that demands total abstinence from eating. The fast is observed for forty-eight hours.

MALTA Beginning at three o'clock in the afternoon, special church services are held. Some towns hold pageants with processions in which life-size statues representing scenes of Christ's Passion and death are portrayed. Local residents walk the parade route dressed in costumes which depict various biblical characters.

ENGLAND Aside from the religious services, observances here are filled with numerous bits of folklore and superstition that relate to the day. Bread baked on this day, for example, is believed to have many curative effects, and good luck is bestowed on sailors who carry it to sea. Good Friday is also thought to be a good time to sow seed, especially parsley. A centuries-old tradition is to play marbles on this day, a custom reminiscent of the Roman soldiers who played dice at the foot of the cross upon which Christ died. In fact, in a couple of areas of England, Good Friday has come to be known as Marbles Day.

AUSTRIA On Good Friday, many Austrians make pilgrimages to shrines or churches, sometimes walking up to ten hours each way.

FINLAND Good Friday is called Long Friday here, just as it is in Sweden and Norway. Traditionally, it is a day for quiet activities, such as reading the Bible. In older times, fasting was strictly enforced, even to the point of denying children and infants milk. Rules relaxed over time so that a simple meat stew could be eaten on Good Friday. As in Germany and Sweden, the parents of West Finland spanked their children in memory of Christ's suffering.

O blasphemous and blind! shall we Rejoice at Eastertide When Christ is risen but to be Recrucified?

Hot Cross Buns

If there is one type of food that is widely associated with Good Friday, it is hot cross buns. We attribute them to England, where they were only eaten on Good Friday and remain a treasured tradition. There are several superstitions attached to the hot cross bun. One superstition has it that one of the buns should be kept in a safe place throughout the year. If illness befell someone, recovery was aided by drinking water into which a little of the bun was grated. Further, there was a notion that if you didn't eat your hot cross bun on Good Friday, your house would burn down. Of course, everyone ate their buns and there were no fires.

INGREDIENTS

1	package dry yeast
¼	cup warm water
3¾	cups all-purpose flour
1	teaspoon cinnamon
1	teaspoon salt
¼	teaspoon ground cloves
¼	teaspoon ground nutmeg
¾	cup milk
½	cup granulated sugar
¼	cup butter
1	egg, beaten
¾	cup currants
2	tablespoons lemon zest
1	egg yolk
1	tablespoon water

DIRECTIONS *(makes 18 buns)*

In a small bowl, soften 1 package dry yeast in ¼ cup warm (120°–130° F) water; set aside. In a large bowl, sift together 3½ cups of the all-purpose flour, 1 teaspoon cinnamon, 1 teaspoon salt, ¼ teaspoon ground cloves, and ¼ teaspoon ground nutmeg. Set aside. In a large saucepan, scald ¾ cup milk; remove from heat and add ½ cup granulated sugar and ¼ cup butter; stir to melt. Cool to lukewarm. Stir in 1 beaten egg and yeast mixture. In a small bowl, sprinkle remaining ¼ cup all-purpose flour over ¾ cup currants. Stir currant mixture into batter along with 2 tablespoons lemon zest. Add flour and spice mixture, stirring to make a soft dough. Turn out on a lightly floured board and let rest 10 minutes. Knead until smooth and elastic, about 5 to 8 minutes. Place in a greased bowl, turning to grease top. Cover and let rise in a warm place until doubled in bulk. Preheat oven to 375° F. Punch down dough and divide into 3 parts. Divide each third into 6 pieces and roll each into a smooth ball. Place on greased baking sheets with sides of balls touching. Cover and let rise in a warm place until doubled in bulk. In a small bowl, beat 1 egg yolk with 1 tablespoon water. Brush over tops of buns. Bake for 10 to 12 minutes or until golden brown. Remove from baking sheets; cool. Spread frosting on top of buns in the form of a cross.

HOT CROSS FROSTING

1 cup powdered sugar
½ teaspoon vanilla
3 tablespoons water

In a small bowl, sift 1 cup powdered sugar. Stir in ½ teaspoon vanilla and water, a tablespoon at a time, until frosting is thick and smooth.

Hot cross buns,
Hot cross buns,
One a penny, two a penny
Hot cross buns.
If you have no daughters,
Give them to your sons,
One a penny, two a penny,
Hot cross buns.

SALISBURY CATHEDRAL
Salisbury, England
David Endersbee/Tony Stone Images

93

The Old Rugged Cross

Words and music by George Bernard

1. On a hill far a-way stood an old rug-ged cross, The em-blem of suf-f'ring and shame; And I love that old cross where the dear-est and best For a world of lost sin-ners was slain.

2. Oh, that old rug-ged cross so de-spised by the world, Has a won-drous at-trac-tion for me; For the dear Lamb of God left His glo-ry a-bove, To bear it to dark Cal-va-ry.

3. In the old rug-ged cross, stained with blood so di-vine, A won-drous beau-ty I see; For 'twas on that old cross Je-sus suf-fered and died, To par-don and sanc-ti-fy me.

4. To the old rug-ged cross I will ev-er be true, Its shame and re-proach glad-ly bear; Then He'll call me some day to my home far a-way, Where His glo-ry for-ev-er I'll share.

So I'll cher-ish the old rug-ged cross, Till my tro-phies at last I lay down; I will cling to the old rug-ged cross, And ex-change it some day for a crown.

cross, the old rug-ged cross,

cross, the old rug-ged cross,

The Cross Was His Own

They borrowed a bed to lay His head
   When Christ the Lord came down;
They borrowed the ass in the mountain pass
   For Him to ride to town;
But the crown that He wore and the cross that He bore
   Were His own—
   The cross was His own.

He borrowed the bread when the crowd He fed
   On the grassy mountainside,
He borrowed the dish of broken fish
   With which He satisfied.
But the crown that He wore and the cross that He bore
   Were His own—
   The cross was His own.

He borrowed the ship in which to sit
   To teach the multitude;
He borrowed a nest in which to rest—
   He had never a home so rude;
But the crown that He wore and the cross that He bore
   Were His own—
   The cross was His own.

He borrowed a room on His way to the tomb
   The Passover lamb to eat;
They borrowed a cave for Him a grave,
   They borrowed a winding sheet.
But the crown that He wore and the cross that He bore
   Were His own—
   The cross was His own.

          Author Unknown

Good Friday

This day upon the bitter tree
Died One who had He willed
Could have dried up the wide sea
   And the wind stilled.

It was about the ninth hour
He surrendered the ghost,
And His face was a faded flower
   Drooping and lost.

Who then was not afraid?
Targeted, heart and eye,
Struck, as with darts, by godhead
   In human agony.

For Him, who with a cry
Could shatter if He willed
The sea and earth and sky
   And them rebuild,

Who chose amid the tumult
Of the darkening sky
A chivalry more difficult—
   As Man to die—

What answering meed of love
Can finite flesh return
That is not all unworthy of
   The God I mourn?
       A. J. M. Smith

The Legend of the Dogwood

INCLUDED IN THE MANY EASTER LEGENDS is that of the dogwood. According to one legend, the dogwood was once tall and strong, not unlike the cedar or oak, and its wood was used to fashion the cross upon which Jesus was to be crucified. The dogwood tree cringed in shame at being used for such a cruel purpose. God promised the dogwood that it would never again be so strong that it could be used for a cross. Thus, the once powerful dogwood tree now grows small and crooked. As a memorial to Jesus' suffering and death, the dogwood blooms grow in the shape of a cross. The petals show the brown and red prints of the nails used for the Crucifixion; a crown of thorns graces the center of each flower. The dogwood is spring's reminder of the death and Resurrection of Jesus.

The Dogwood Tree

In Jesus' time the dogwood grew
To a stately size and a lovely hue.
'Twas strong and firm as oak branches interwoven;
For the cross of Christ its timber was chosen.
Seeing the distress at this use of its wood,
Christ made a promise that still holds good.
"Never again shall the dogwood grow
Large enough to be used so.
It shall be slender and twisted be
With blossoms like the cross for all to see.
As bloodstains the petals marked in brown;
The blossom's center shall wear a thorny crown.
All who see it will remember Me,
Crucified on a cross from the dogwood tree.
Cherished and protected this tree shall be,
A reminder to all of My agony."

Author Unknown

WHITE AND PINK FLOWERING DOGWOOD TREES
Greenfield, Connecticut
Johnson's Photography

97

More Easter Legends

The Snowdrop in purest
*   white arraie*
First rears her hedde on
*   Candelmass daie:*
While the Crocus hastens
*   to the shrine*
Of Primrose lone on
*   S. Valentine.*
Then comes the Daffodil
*   beside*
Our Ladye's Smock at our
*   Ladye's tide;*
Aboute S. George, when
*   blue is worn,*
The blue Harebells the
*   field adorn.*
Against the daie of the
*   Holie Cross,*
The Crowfoot gilds the
*   flowrie grass.*
The Passion-flower long
*   has blowed,*
To betoken us signs of the
*   holie rood.*
*   Author Unknown*

CHRISTIAN SYMBOLISM is often found in legends about flowers. The passionflower is so named because it symbolizes the Passion of Christ. According to a Spanish legend, it is believed that after Christ was crucified, the kindly passionflower grew to cover the cross and the marks left in its wood by the nails. Spanish missionaries working in what is now Latin America discovered the passionflower growing wild and took its existence as proof that the natives should be converted.

The passionflower has ten petals, representing the ten faithful apostles, thus excluding Judas and Peter. The purple threads emanating from the center symbolize the crown of thorns; the center represents the three nails. One of the stamens represents a hammer; the remaining four form the cross. Curiously, the time that it takes for the flower to bloom is three days. After it was brought to Europe, it acquired other names. In Europe it is called Jesus' Passion, Our Lord's Flower, Crown of Thorns, and Mother of God's Star, to name but a few examples.

MANY SPRING FLOWERS and several trees have a place in the Easter folklore tradition of Germany. In the Black Forest early spring blooms, as well as grasses and various kinds of foliage, were made into crosses and hearts and carried to church to be blessed. It was believed that the pear tree provided the wood of the cross, and as a result the wood later developed roots and produced red flowers as well as leaves and fruit that were similarly veined. The glossy-leaved holly, commonly called English holly (*Ilex aquifolium*), had its white fruits changed to red when a drop of the blood of Christ fell on them. An old German myth had it that Judas, overtaken by remorse, ended his life by hanging himself from the branches of a tall brier rose. The red fruits of this thorny bush were called Judas berries, and presumably the bush was a small tree in form.

Daniel Foley

IN IRELAND the story is told of a robin that flew close to Jesus as he hung upon the cross on Good Friday. Seeing the hawthorn crown upon Jesus' head, the robin plucked out a thorn. Blood flowed from the wound and fell upon the robin's breast. To this day the robin's breast is marked with the color of Christ's blood in remembrance of the kindness of the sympathetic bird.

PEAR TREES IN BLOOM
Mount Hood, Oregon
Dick Dietrich/Dietrich Photography

The Pietà

N ow there stood by the cross of Jesus his mother. . . . When Jesus therefore saw his mother, and the disciple standing by, whom he loved, he saith unto his mother, Woman, behold thy son! Then saith he to the disciple, Behold thy mother! And from that hour that disciple took her unto his own home.

John 19:25–27

Observation

The Virgin-Mother stood at
   distance (there)
From her Son's Cross, not
   shedding once a tear:
Because the Law forbade
   to sit and cry
For those, who did as
   malefactors die.
Observe we may, how
   Mary Joses then,
And th' other Mary
   (Mary Magdalen)
Sat by the grave; and sadly
   sitting there,
Shed for their Master many
   a bitter tear:
But 'twas not till their dearest
   Lord was dead;
And then to weep they both
   were licensed.

Robert Herrick

PIETÀ
Michelangelo Buonarroti
Vatican Museums and Galleries, Rome, Italy
Canali PhotoBank, Milan/SuperStock

MICHELANGELO BUONARROTI was born in Florence, Italy, in 1475. As a boy, Michelangelo was raised in genteel poverty by a family who had no regard for his talent or aspirations as an artist. In fact, his father would beat him for bringing shame to their family by pursuing a career in the arts. At the age of thirteen, however, Michelangelo began his formal training in Florence as an artist.

At the age of twenty-three, Michelangelo received a commission to sculpt a Pietà, which is the Italian word for "pity" and is applied to a painting or sculpture depicting Mary supporting the dead body of her son on her lap. The theme originated in the early fourteenth century in Germany, where it was called *Vesperbild.*

The sculpture, which is today in St. Peter's Basilica in Rome, took one year to complete. The magnificent and deeply moving portrayal of Mary holding her dead son in her lap astonished all who laid eyes on it. Critics doubted the ability of one so young to create such masterful work. Rumor abounded as to the identity of the sculptor who could have created this masterpiece. So Michelangelo quietly returned to St. Peter's and chiseled these words into the piece of art: MICHELANGELUS•BONARO-TUS•FLORENT•FACIEBAT: Michelangelo Buonarroti of Florence made this. The Pietà is the only one of his works he signed. From that day on, his genius spoke for itself.

For God So Loved the World

Music by John Stainer

God so loved the world, God so loved the

world, that He gave His on-ly be-got-ten Son, that

who-so be-liev-eth, be-liev-eth in Him Should not per-ish,

should not per-ish, but have ev-er-last-ing life. For God

sent not His Son in-to the world to con-demn the world; God sent not His

For God So Loved the World

Son in-to the world to con-demn the world; But that the world through

Him might be sav - ed.

2.

life, ev-er-last-ing life, ev-er-last-ing,

ev - er - last - ing life; God

so loved the world, God so loved the world,

God so loved the world.

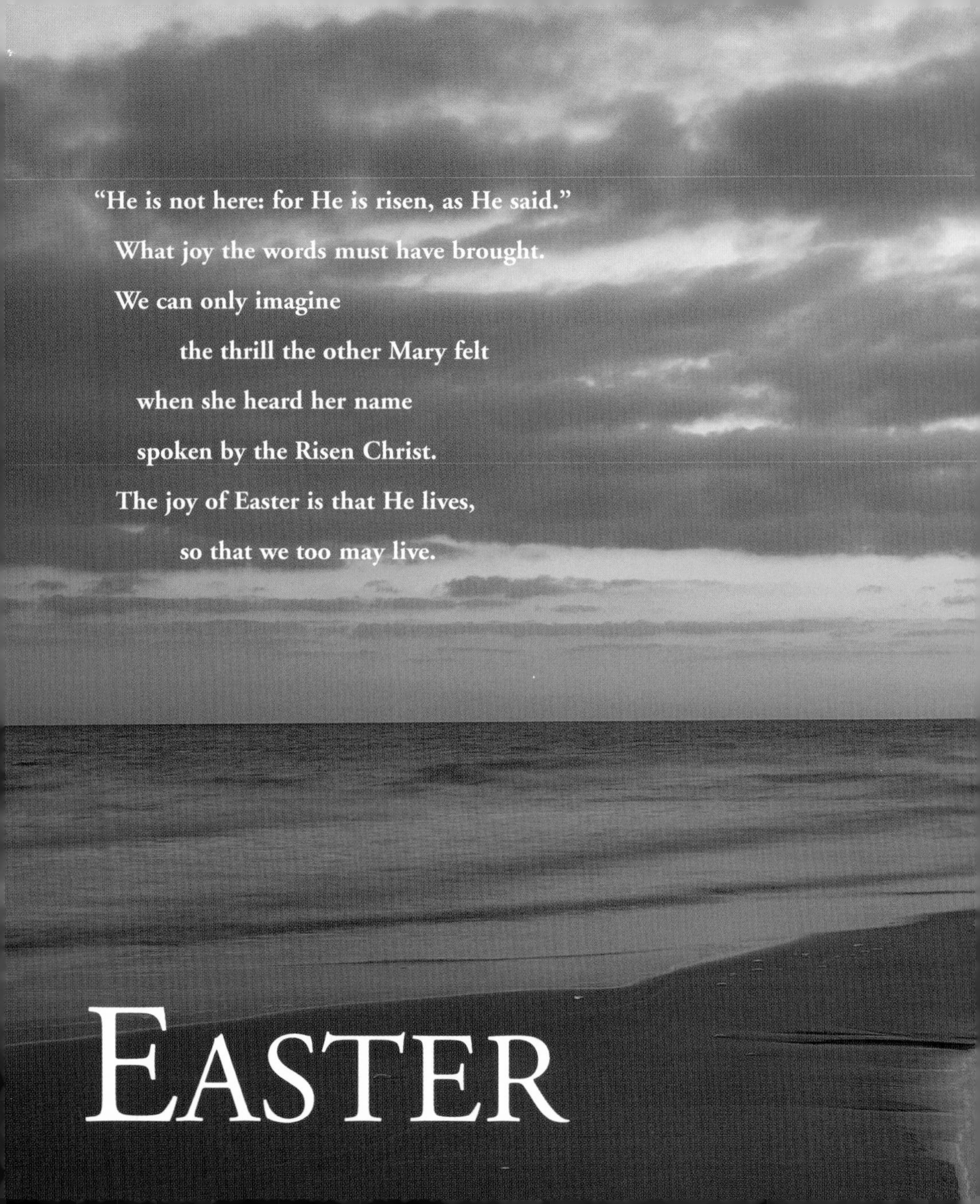

"He is not here: for He is risen, as He said."

What joy the words must have brought.

We can only imagine

the thrill the other Mary felt

when she heard her name

spoken by the Risen Christ.

The joy of Easter is that He lives,

so that we too may live.

EASTER

The Light of the World

*I*n him was life; and the life was the light of men. And the light shineth in darkness; and the darkness comprehended it not. . . . He was in the world, and the world was made by him, and the world knew him not. He came unto his own, and his own received him not. But as many as received him, to them gave he power to become the sons of God, even to them that believe on his name: Which were born, not of blood, nor of the will of the flesh, nor of the will of man, but of God. And the Word was made flesh, and dwelt among us, (and we beheld his glory, the glory as of the only begotten of the Father,) full of grace and truth.

John 1:4–5, 10–14

Morning Has Broken

Morning has broken like the first morning;
Blackbird has spoken like the first bird.
Praise for the singing! Praise for the morning!
Praise for them springing fresh from the Word.

Sweet the rain's new fall, sunlit from heaven,
Like the first dewfall on the first grass.
Praise for the sweetness of the wet garden,
Sprung in completeness where His feet pass.

Mine is the sunlight, mine is the morning,
Born of the one light Eden saw play.
Praise with elation, praise every morning,
God's recreation of the new day.

Eleanor Farjeon

*Lord, in the morning thou shalt hear
My voice ascending high.*
Isaac Watts

SUNRISE OVER SNOW-COVERED PEAKS
Bernese Oberland, Switzerland
Joe Cornish/Tony Stone Images

THE EASTER SUNRISE SERVICE

The barrier stone has rolled away,
And loud the angels sing;
The Christ comes forth this blessed day
To reign, a deathless King.

For shall we not believe He lives
Through such awakening?
Behold, how God each April gives
The miracle of Spring.
Edwin L. Sabin

EASTER DAWN OR SUNRISE SERVICES are characteristic of Easter in America. The first spot in the continental United States which is hit by the Easter sun is Cadillac Mountain in Acadia National Park, just outside Bar Harbor, Maine. Every year worshippers shiver in the cool morning sunlight and raise their alleluias in the often frosty air.

At least nineteen national parks have Easter sunrise services. In Aspen, Colorado, worshippers travel by ski lift. Red Rocks Amphitheater outside Denver was built particularly for these services, though it is used now for concerts as well. Garden of the Gods in Colorado Springs has a famous dawn service that has long been carried on network radio, as has the Grand Canyon, Soldier Field in Chicago, Cathedral of the Pines in Rindge, New Hampshire, Yosemite National Park, and the Hollywood Bowl in California.

There is a service at Lincoln's birthplace in Hodgenville, Kentucky, and another on the steps of the Capitol in Salt Lake City. The service at the Tomb of the Unknown Soldier in Arlington National Cemetery, near Washington, D.C., attracts people from great distances. The last sunrise service of the morning is held in the crater of a passive volcano at Punchbowl National Memorial Cemetery outside Honolulu.

Nearly every town and city in the United States has several such early services, usually in a spot of beauty out-of-doors. One well-known indoor service is held at New York City's mammoth Radio City Music Hall, sponsored by the city's Protestant Council. But Central Park also is the scene of a sunrise service, as are many smaller parks around the city. In Columbus, Ohio, the Conservatory at the Botanic Gardens provides an outdoor jungle setting with warm comfort. At Tampa, Florida, where the cold morning air is no problem, a special feature of one service is the releasing of thirty-three white pigeons. In Lawton, Oklahoma, a six-hour pageant from midnight to dawn showing the life of Christ is climaxed by the reenactment of the Resurrection. The project began in 1926 with a group from the Congregational Church.

The claim for the first Easter sunrise service in this country is made by Spanish explorers who conducted a service on their ship anchored off California on Easter of 1609. But it is more likely that the custom was brought to the U.S. by the Moravians, who settled in Winston-Salem, North Carolina, in 1773. The Moravian Easter customs, still kept in such strong settlements as Bethlehem, Pennsylvania, and Winston-Salem, and even in tiny Gnaddenhutten, Ohio, are most picturesque and in keeping with the spirit of the day.

For these Moravian services, young people are up at 3:30 A.M., loosening up their trombones. While it is still quite dark they begin playing Easter hymns from the belfry of the church, with another group answering from the parsonage steps. This antiphonal brass choir music and playing through the dark streets of the town goes on until nearly daylight. The people, aroused by the music, hurry before 5:00 to the church, where the only illumination comes from a lighted cross surrounded by palms on the altar. When it is time for the service to begin, the minister rushes into the darkened church and shouts, "The Lord is risen!" The congregation rises to its feet to respond, "He is risen indeed!"—much in the same manner as in the Greek Orthodox Church. Lights come on and a ritual service follows. Then the entire congregation walks to the graveyard where another brief service is held. Finally, they return to the church for breakfast, which has been prepared by a men's group.

Easter sunrise services are supposed to have originated in the Middle Ages, when very early on Easter morning joyful voices, the boom of cannon, and the clanging of bells announced the happy news, "Christ is risen!" Even older traditions of dancing to welcome the sun or getting up to watch the angels dance existed in Europe. In fact, elderly people in France used to say that the first few persons to see the sun on Easter morning would see angels dancing in the new rays that extended into the dark sky.

Rachel Hartman

People and realms of
    ev'ry tongue
And infant voices shall
    proclaim
Their early blessings on
    his Name.

Blessings abound where'er
    he reigns;
The pris'ner leaps to loose
    his chains;
The weary find
    eternal rest,
And all who suffer want
    are blest.

Let every creature rise
    and bring
Blessing and honor to
    our King;
Angels descend with
    songs again,
And earth repeat the loud
    Amen.
        Isaac Watts

Arise, New Hope Awaits–
Sleepers, Awake!

And, behold, I come quickly; and my reward is with me, to give every man according as his work shall be. I am Alpha and Omega, the beginning and the end, the first and the last. Blessed are they that do his commandments, that they may have right to the tree of life, and may enter in through the gates into the city. . . . I Jesus have sent mine angel to testify unto you these things in the churches. I am the root and the offspring of David, and the bright and morning star.

Revelation 22:12–14, 16

The custom of greeting the rising sun with hallelujahs began in early Christian times. The word was taken from the Hebrew Hallelu Yah, *an exclamation of praise or joy meaning "Praise His Holy Name." The Resurrection of Christ is, therefore, an optimum setting for this lovely custom.*

Because hallelujahs are generally omitted from church music during Lent, this is a welcome return to the triumphant rejoicing of the Easter season.

WHEN I WAS GROWING UP in Danville, Virginia, attending the Easter Sunday sunrise service in the quaint Moravian restoration of Old Salem in Winston-Salem, North Carolina, was a tradition. Cars and buses full of worshippers started out in the dark of night to arrive in the village just in time to see the lights in the old brick and timber houses come on as the sleeping town was awakened to a rousing chorus of "Sleepers, Awake!" played by a magnificent brass band.

While the moon was still high, thousands of visitors of every sect, creed, and race paraded from the steps of the Home Church, where they had gathered, to the nearby resting place of the Moravian dead, God's Acre, as Moravian cemeteries are called. When all were assembled, prayers were given and songs were sung, and antiphonal brass choruses were played while everyone awaited the dawning of Easter morn.

Silently and wondrously the bright moon that had lighted the worshippers' way slowly began to lose its glow as the sky turned from pitch black to an azure blue. Silently and wondrously a soft yellow-pink glow spread across the earth. Then in a sudden burst from behind the majestic, newly budded and leafed trees in the east, the sun appeared.

In that emotionally charged moment the benediction was pronounced: "Go forth!" In the distance the last deep, compelling tones of

the brass horns hung in the morning mist, bringing, for another year, the sacred service to an end. Yet few of the worshippers left. Peacefully, reverently, the guests lingered, wanting the moment, the morning, and the peace to last.

Emyl Jenkins

THE GRAND CANYON
Arizona
William Johnson/
Johnson's Photography

Easter Fire

WHEN SAINT PATRICK was a boy somewhere in what is now England or Scotland, he was captured by pirates and taken to Ireland. For six years he tended sheep; then he escaped to France and became a monk. In A.D. 432, a vision led him back to Ireland as a missionary.

Like other pagans, the Irish held spring fire rites, and they did not want to give them up. So, in place of the old custom, Patrick offered them a Christian fire rite. On Easter Eve he gathered them together for huge bonfires outside the churches.

As the years passed, they began preparing their homes for the new Easter fire in special ways. No fire or light burned in a house on Easter Saturday. All candlesticks, lamps, and stoves had to be clean and ready for the sacred fire. During Easter week, a boy in the family would place a log with others lying in a huge pile beside the church. Then on Easter Eve, the priest struck fire from flint and set the logs ablaze. Each boy found his own log and pulled it out by a wire he had left fastened to the end. Swinging it around in the air, he ran home.

With the burning log, his family would light all the lamps and candles and touch off the kindling in the fireplace or stove. In many European villages, people still carry home sticks lighted at the new Easter fire. In others the Easter flames are often taken home in lanterns.

Easter fires are a symbol of life and light, which triumph over death and darkness.

Edna Barth

SALISBURY CATHEDRAL AT SUNRISE
Salisbury, England
Suzanne and Nick Geary/Tony Stone Images

EASTER
SUNDAY
AROUND
THE
WORLD

For, lo, the winter is past,

the rain is over and gone;

The flowers appear on the

earth; the time of the

singing of birds is come,

and the voice of the turtle

is heard in our land; The

fig tree putteth forth her

green figs, and the vines

with the tender grape give

a good smell.

Song of Solomon 2:11-13

SPAIN As in many other parts of the world, the high point of the liturgical calendar in Spain is not the birth of Jesus, but the Easter Resurrection signifying Jesus' triumph over death and the promise of eternal life. The respect that the Spanish people pay to Easter and the week prior to it are evidenced by the thousands of processions and pageants staged during Holy Week. This continues into Easter Sunday all over Spain.

In Catalonia, traditional Easter hymns, called *caramelles,* are sung in the street. Many ceremonies are based on the emotional reunion between the Resurrected Christ and His mother, Mary. In a procession featuring people chosen to represent Jesus and His mother, thousands of multicolored streamers are thrown from balconies as the two figures pass. Outdoor festivals are common and are held into Easter Monday and Tuesday.

GREECE On Easter Sunday in the village of Castellorizo, services are held at the monastery, high above the town. Children carry fat candles, at the base of which they have fashioned paper ornamental cutouts to catch the drippings. The men sit on one side, the women on the other. Chants are given while the congregation chats with one another and the children run in endless circles.

Gail Chase

IRAN Easter comes in the spring when the land is a vast carpet of wild flowers. The festival is celebrated in the home, the orchards, and the hayfields. Joy and happiness reign supreme for a whole week. The people dress up in their best attire and pay visits. They greet each other by saying, "May your Easter be a blessing." Each day is given over to a different program. The first day of the festival is a visiting day, the second day is for running and ball-playing. The third and fourth days they match colored eggs and play games. The final day the fun reaches its climax, as all these various pleasures are enjoyed together. They play, run, dance, and the boys have wrestling matches. The young people enjoy themselves to such an extent that for a week after they are heartbroken because the festival is over.

Yovel B. Mirza

CZECHOSLOVAKIA Easter is the most joyous holiday of the year. Friends exchange eggs with the greeting "Christ is risen" and the reply "He is risen indeed." Flowers and eggs abound in markets, homes, and churches. In times past, the most beautiful egg painted by a boy or girl was saved for a special best-loved person. It was very often a pre-engagement symbol. Young people on the farm carried their eggs in a basket, delivering them from farmhouse to farmhouse. One story tells of a young man who decorated an egg tree below the window of his loved one. On Easter morning there it was, to her surprise. Trees in the yard or garden were sometimes decorated. Another ancient custom occurred on Easter Saturday afternoon when the village boys collected and stacked wood and placed a straw-covered cross in the center of that stack. After an evening church service, the boys would light lanterns at the Paschal Candle, hurry to the stack of wood, and set fire to the cross.

Pat Martin

ETHIOPIA Easter is called *Fasika* and is the last of the major feast days of the Ethiopian year. It actually takes place about two weeks later than in Western churches. Easter is spent in quiet pursuits, such as reading or playing board games. The Easter service begins at midnight and continues until dawn, which the Ethiopians consider to be the beginning of the day. Easter feasts begin after church and continue into Easter Monday and longer.

RUSSIA In the Eastern Church, Easter is the high point of the Russian festival year. As in Western churches, the time is a celebration of the rebirth and regeneration of life. This is particularly meaningful in a land that has lain under snow and ice for many months. The Easter Eve service finds Russians standing for several hours during a long traditional ritual. The old tradition describes a darkened church which is lit with hundreds of candles at midnight. Just after midnight, the Lenten fast is finally broken with a special meal. The greeting at this meal is "Christ is risen." The response is "He is risen indeed."

The year's at the spring

And day's at the morn;

Morning's at seven;

The hillside's dew-pearled;

The lark's on the wing;

The snail's on the thorn;

God's in his heaven—

All's right with the world!

Robert Browning

Hosanna to the

son of David:

Blessed is he that cometh

in the name of the Lord;

Hosanna in the highest.

Matthew 21:9

Of Dates, Parades, Clothes, and Cards

Day!

Faster and more fast,
O'er night's brim, day boils
    at last;
Boils, pure gold, o'er the
    cloud-cap's brim
Where spurting and suppressed
    it lay,
For not a froth-flake touched
    the rim
Of yonder gap in the solid gray
Of the eastern cloud, an
    hour away;
But forth one wavelet, then
    another, curled,
Till the whole sunrise, not to
    be suppressed,
Rose, reddened, and its
    seething breast
Flickered in bounds, grew gold,
Then overflowed the world.
        Robert Browning

EASTER AS WE KNOW IT today has developed from a long history. Early Christians for a time used the Jewish Passover time as the day of the Easter celebration. Hence, the word *Pesach,* or Passover, evolved into other names for Easter. In France, it is called *Pâques;* in Sweden, *Pask;* in Greece, *Pascha;* and in the Netherlands, it is *Paach.*

Easter day has no specific reference in the Bible. More correctly it is the day of Christ's Resurrection. The use of the word Easter began only about 1400 years ago as the early Christians were trying to gain greater acceptance of Christianity throughout the Western world. To do this, they chose to use the word referring to the ancient spring celebration of the goddess *Eostre.* This, they thought, would be more acceptable to the people they were trying to convert.

This is underscored by the many ways that Easter and the days leading up to it are observed. From raucous reveling to prayerful piety, the customs and traditions associated with this time are numerous and very diverse. Much of any country's tradition is based on local customs and thus is steeped in both religious symbolism and native folklore.

One thing is absolute, however. Easter—in any language—is meant to be a celebration of the Resurrection from the dead of Jesus Christ.

Up until A.D. 325, the date of Easter was the same as the Jewish Passover. Since Christ was crucified during Passover, the two celebrations coincided. It was at the Council of Nicaea in that year that a new dating system was devised. Easter would be the Sunday following the first full moon after the vernal equinox—the one day in spring when day and night are each twelve hours long—usually March 21 or 22. The seemingly complicated system is dependent on the timing of this full moon, and causes Easter to fall anywhere between March 22 and April 25.

THE U.S. has been credited with three great contributions to Easter folklore—the Easter parade, religious sunrise services, and the sending of cheery Easter cards. Each tradition began in Europe, of course, and has made its way through the culture of the Europeans who brought their traditions to this country.

EASTER CARDS developed from the custom of exchanging colored eggs at Easter as good-luck pieces. Pictures of eggs were substituted about 1850 in Germany, and later, religious scenes were used. The custom of sending Easter greetings by picture postcard became popular in the United States in the 1870s when postcard publishers inaugurated lighthearted designs. The postcard vogue lasted until about 1910, when present-day greeting cards with envelopes became more widely used.

EASTER PARADES after church services survive from a much earlier time. In northern Europe, people paraded through the countryside in celebration of the coming new year and the promise of spring. They wore new clothes in celebration of the "new clothes" donned by the earth.

NEW CLOTHES at Easter probably dates back to when the New Year started in March and new clothes were worn to signify a new beginning. Some people trace it to the early Christian times when white robes were conferred on the recently baptized. According to this belief, the regular members of the church wore new attire in memory of their own earlier baptisms. Wearing new clothes on Easter sometimes even was held as a superstition. In the United States it came to mean that wearing three new items of clothing on Easter would bring good luck throughout the year. In Italy the custom of new clothes was taken so seriously that if a suitor sent gloves to a girl on Easter, it was taken as a sign of serious intention. If the girl wore the gloves, a wedding was in store. As for the traditional Easter bonnet, it actually originated as a bouquet of flowers worn during these ancient celebrations.

Evensong

The embers of the day are red
Beyond the murky hill.
The kitchen smokes; the bed
In the darkling house is spread:
The great sky darkens overhead,
And the great woods are shrill.
So far have I been led,
Lord, by Thy will:
So far have I followed, Lord,
	and wondered still.
The breeze from the
	embalmed land
Blows sudden towards the shore,
And claps my cottage door.
I hear the signal, Lord—
	I understand.
The night at Thy command
Comes. I will eat and sleep and
	will not question more.
		Robert Louis Stevenson

Egg rolling is another favorite American custom that, too, began centuries ago in Europe. The unique celebration and egg rolling at the White House lawn on Easter Monday originated directly from the Monday celebrations of the Europeans. The custom is thought to be symbolic of the rolling away of the stone from Christ's tomb.

Russian Kulich

In the Ukraine, the Easter celebration sometimes continues until the Thursday following Easter. In addition to kulich, *another traditional dish of the day is* pashka, *a delicate dessert made of cream cheese, butter, and sour cream, along with dried fruit and almonds.*

INGREDIENTS

1 package active dry yeast

¼ cup very warm water

1½ cups milk, scalded and cooled

5½ to 6 cups all-purpose flour

4 egg yolks

⅔ cup sugar

¼ cup lemon-flavored instant tea

1 teaspoon water

1 cup butter, melted

⅔ cup blanched almonds, chopped

⅓ cup lemon zest

¼ teaspoon salt

⅓ cup seedless golden raisins

DIRECTIONS *(makes 2 loaves)*

Sprinkle yeast over warm water and set aside. Prepare 2 clean 46-ounce juice cans. Cut brown paper to fit bottoms and sides. Grease paper and line insides of cans. In a large bowl, combine milk and 4 cups of the flour. Stir yeast mixture into flour mixture. Cover and let rise in a warm place until doubled in bulk (1 to 2 hours). In a small bowl, combine egg yolks and sugar; beat until light-colored. In a small bowl, mix tea with 1 teaspoon water. Add to dough along with melted butter, almonds, lemon zest, salt, and raisins. Blend thoroughly. Stir in enough flour to make a dough. Turn out onto a floured surface; knead in remaining flour until dough is smooth and no longer sticky. Divide dough in half. Place dough halves in prepared cans. Cover and let rise in a warm place until doubled in bulk. Preheat oven to 375° F. Bake bread 1 hour and 15 minutes or until tops are brown. Cover tops with foil to prevent overbrowning. Cool in cans 5 minutes. Turn out onto racks to cool. Stand bread upright and drizzle with Lemon Glaze.

LEMON GLAZE

½ cup powdered sugar

2 teaspoons hot water

1 teaspoon lemon juice

In a small bowl, combine all ingredients. Blend well.

Easter Egg Bread

European countries, and those along the Mediterranean especially, in one form or another have a traditional recipe for a festive bread decorated with dyed eggs. Children especially enjoy this treat, since the eggs magically bake along with the bread.

INGREDIENTS

2 packages active dry yeast
½ cup warm water
½ cup milk
½ cup sugar
1 teaspoon salt
½ cup vegetable shortening
  Zest of 2 lemons
2 eggs, lightly beaten
4 cups sifted all-purpose flour
1 egg, lightly beaten
  Multicolored candy
    sprinkles
12 uncooked dyed eggs

DIRECTIONS *(makes 2 braided rings)*

In a small bowl, dissolve yeast in warm water (110° to 115° F). In a large saucepan, scald milk. Add sugar, salt, shortening, and lemon zest. Cool to lukewarm. Stir in yeast mixture. Add 2 eggs and 2½ cups of the flour. Beat until smooth. Stir in enough flour, a little at a time, until dough can be handled. Turn dough out onto a floured surface; knead in remaining flour until smooth and elastic. Place dough in a lightly greased bowl; turn dough to grease top. Cover and let rise in a warm, draft-free place until doubled in bulk. Punch dough down. Cover and let rise until almost doubled in bulk. Divide dough into 6 portions. Shape each into a 30-inch rope on a lightly floured surface. Place three of the ropes on a lightly greased baking sheet. Braid loosely and form into a ring. Repeat for remaining three ropes of dough. Place 6 eggs in braid of each ring. Cover and let rise until doubled in bulk. Brush tops with beaten egg. Sprinkle with candy sprinkles. Preheat oven to 375° F. Bake braids 20 minutes or until lightly browned. Remove to wire racks to cool slightly before serving.

EASTER LIGHTS THE WORLD

Heavenly sunlight,

Heavenly sunlight,

Flooding my soul

with glory divine:

Hallelujah,

I am rejoicing,

Singing His praises,

Jesus is mine.

ITALY On Easter Saturday, a crowd gathers around an oxcart loaded with fireworks, standing ready beside a church. Suddenly a firecracker in the shape of a dove flies out of the church window above and runs down over a wire to the oxcart. The fireworks explode and the firecracker dove races back up the wire and into the church. If the "bird" reaches the altar before exploding, there will be shouts of joy, and everybody present will expect good luck in the coming year.

TAXCO, MEXICO A structure one hundred feet high is built out of reeds just to hold the Easter fireworks. Everybody gathers to watch. One firework sets off another, and as they explode in turn with beautiful colors, they form the shapes of crosses, animals, flowers, and birds.

ITALY, SPAIN, PORTUGAL, AND LATIN AMERICA The explosions of light and cheerful noise of Easter fireworks all express joy and are one more way of saying: Out of darkness comes light, and with it, new hope and new life.

SWEDEN Swedish children draw pictures of witches and write Easter greetings on them. Then, dressed up like witches themselves, they put their "Easter letters" in the mailboxes of their friends and set off firecrackers in the street. The witches stand for evil spirits; the noisy firecrackers are meant to frighten them away.

Edna Barth

THE EASTER CANDLE The earliest celebrations of Easter in Jerusalem featured a ceremony known as the "Illumination": the lighting of a candle at the beginning of the Easter Vigil or Night Watch on the eve of Easter Sunday. The blessing of the new fire and the lighting of the Paschal candle is an adaptation of this ancient rite. As far back as the fourth century, a large candle decorated with five grains of incense (symbolizing the five wounds that Jesus received on the cross) was blessed on Easter Eve and lit with newly blessed fire to symbolize Christ and spiritual illumination.

In Roman Catholic and other Christian churches, the Paschal candle usually stands at the side of the altar during the Easter service. Placed there on Holy Saturday (the day before Easter), it is removed on Ascension Day and brought back for a final appearance on Pentecost.

In medieval times, parishes would compete with each other to see who could make the largest Paschal candle. One used in 1517 at the altar in Salisbury, England, measured more than thirty feet high. A giant candle made in 1558 for the altar at Westminster Abbey in London required 300 pounds of wax. After Pentecost, the huge candles were usually melted down and made into narrow tapers for funerals of the poor.

Sue Ellen Thompson

CZECHOSLOVAKIA Down through the ages people have commemorated in festival and story the reawakening of nature in the spring. The Czechoslovakian legend about the sun, the moon, and the rooster dates from pagan times in old Slovakia, but like other cherished myths and traditions has become a part of the Czechoslovakian celebration of Easter. The story is told to children shortly before Easter as the traditional decorations are placed on an Easter egg tree:

One day the sun and the moon and a little rooster went out walking. The sun said to the moon, "Why don't you and the rooster look after the sheep for a while?" and nodded toward the stars that studded the sky. The moon was lazy and left the job to the rooster. But the rooster was too weak and the star-sheep ended up in a tangle. Angered at this, the moon seized the rooster by its bright red comb and threw him to the earth. So today the rooster is always afraid of the moon. He calls his family up on the tree in the late afternoon, and early in the morning he shouts to tell the world he is glad his friend the sun is coming back.

On Easter morn,

On Easter morn,

The sun comes

dancing up the sky.

His light leaps up;

It shakes and swings,

Bewildering the

dazzled eye.

On Easter morn

All earth is glad;

The waves rejoice in

the bright sea.

Be still and listen

To your heart,

And hear it beating

merrily!

Elizabeth Coatsworth

Easter Morn

Say, Earth, why hast thou got thee new attire,
And stick'st thy habit full of daisies red?
Seems that thou dost to some high thought aspire,
And some new-found-out bridegroom mean'st to wed;
Tell me, ye trees, so fresh apparellèd,–
   So never let the spiteful canker waste you,
   So never let the heavens with lightning blast you—
Why go you now so trimly dressed, or whither haste you?

Answer me, Jordan, why thy crooked tide
So often wanders from his nearest way,
As though some other way thy stream would slide,
And fain salute the place where something lay.
And you, sweet birds that, shaded from the ray,
   Sit carolling and piping grief away,
   The while the lambs to hear you, dance and play,
Tell me, sweet birds, what is it you so fain would say?

And thou, fair spouse of earth, that every year
Gett'st such a numerous issue of thy bride,
How chance thou hotter shin'st, and draw'st more near?
Sure thou somewhere some worthy sight has spied,
That in one place for joy thou canst not bide:
   And you, dead swallows, that so lively now
   Through the flit air your wingèd passage row,
How could new life into your frozen ashes flow?

Ye primroses and purple violets,
Tell me, why blaze ye from your leavy bed,
And woo men's hands to rent you from your sets,
As though you would somewhere be carrièd,
With fresh perfumes, and velvets garnishèd?
   But ah! I need not ask, 'tis surely so,
   You all would to your Saviour's triumphs go,
There would ye all await, and humble homage do.

                     Giles Fletcher

ROLLING HILLS AND BLOOMING DOGWOOD
Blue Ridge Parkway, North Carolina
William H. Johnson/Johnson's Photography

The Music of Easter

FROM THE VERY EARLIEST TIMES, whenever people gathered together to worship, singing played an important part. Music has always been one way of creating a feeling of unity. For example, there is nothing that so stirs an assembly of persons to patriotism as singing its national anthem. Music has the power to make one feel either sad or joyful.

When congregations first began to worship together in Christ's name it was quite natural, therefore, that music would be a part of the service. As time went on, different kinds of music developed. There were chants which were sung by the priests and the choirs as part of the service itself. There were the great oratorios and Passion music performed by trained singers and accompanied by organ and orchestra.

It is not known who wrote many of the early hymns. Probably they were changed from time to time and are quite different now from the time in which they were first written. Oratorios and Passion music were a later development of church music. Father Philip Neri, a priest who lived in Italy around the middle of the sixteenth century, is given credit for composing the first oratorio.

Father Neri was holding a series of daily meetings in a small chapel of the church called the oratory. In order to make these meetings more interesting and to attract more people to them, Father Neri arranged for certain scenes of the Bible to be reenacted, accompanied by hymn singing. And from that time on, whenever music was used with a dramatized Bible story it was called an oratorio, taking its name from the place where it was first performed.

Passion music was developed first in Germany. Although it, too, was a combination of Bible stories and music, it differed from the oratorio in that it kept within one theme—the Crucifixion and the Resurrection of our Lord. Oratorios are sometimes given in places other than churches, but Passion music is so sacred in nature that it is never performed except in a church.

Janette Woolsey

Christ the Lord Is Risen Today

Words by Charles Wesley • From *Lyra Davidica*

1. Christ the Lord is risen to-day,
2. Lives a-gain our glo-rious King,
3. Love's re-deem-ing work is done,
4. Soar we now where Christ has led,

Al - - - le - lu - ia!

Sons of men and an-gels say,
Where, O Death, is now thy sting?
Fought the fight, the bat-tle won,
Fol-low-ing our ex-alt-ed Head,

Al - - - le - lu - ia!

Raise your joys and tri-umphs high,
Dy-ing once He all doth save,
Death in vain for-bids Him rise,
Made like Him, like Him we rise,

Al - - - le - lu - ia!

Sing, ye heavens, and earth, re-ply,
Where thy vic-to-ry, O Grave?
Christ hath o-pened Par-a-dise,
Ours the cross, the grave, the skies,

Al - - - le - lu - ia!

George Frederick Handel

GEORGE FREDERICK HANDEL was born in Halle, Saxony, on February 23, 1685. His father was ambitious for his son and had plans for him to study law. But young George Frederick had other ideas. From the time he was very young he could think of nothing but music.

By the time he was eighteen, having given law a try, he was convinced that it definitely was not for him. So he withdrew from the university, resigned his church position, and departed for Hamburg. At Hamburg he had no trouble in securing a position as second violinist in the Opera House.

The year 1707 found Handel touring Italy, going first to Florence, then to Rome, and finally to Venice. After three years of travel he decided to settle in Hanover.

The Elector of Hanover was Georg Ludwig. He was very fond of music and became interested in the young talented musician who was establishing such a reputation for himself. But Handel was not ready to settle down yet and was anxious to visit England. So Georg Ludwig gave him permission to do so, and he stayed in that country for a year.

In 1712, Handel again asked for and received permission to revisit England. This time somehow the visit lengthened out, and he was to make London his home until his death forty-six years later.

Handel's life was a succession of ups and downs. Sometimes he was popular, and sometimes his popularity seemed to be in a decline. In 1741, attendance at his operas became so small that they were discontinued. On April 8 of that year he gave his last operatic concert.

It was in August that same year that he began working on *Messiah.* The Bible verses that were used as a text for this oratorio were chosen for him by Charles Jennens Jr.

Handel was particularly inspired by the selection of verses Jennens gave him. Working feverishly, he finished composing the music within twenty-three days. Legend has said that one time when a servant brought him food he found the composer working on what was to be the "Hallelujah Chorus" with tears streaming down his cheeks.

Messiah was performed first in Dublin, April 13, 1742. The notices sent out prior to the opening requested ladies not to wear hoops and gentlemen to leave their swords at home. Evidently space was at a premium, and hoops and swords took up too much room!

On Wednesday, March 23, 1743, at the Theatre Royal in Covent Garden, London, King George II was among those in attendance at the first English performance of George Frederick Handel's oratorio *Messiah*.

Handel himself was conducting, and as the music reached its great climax in the singing of the "Hallelujah Chorus," the king was so moved by its magnificence that he rose to his feet. Since no Englishman remains seated when his monarch is standing, everyone in the audience arose too. And thus was the tradition established of standing during the rendition of the "Hallelujah Chorus" of *Messiah*.

Although the first London performance was a great success, *Messiah* did not prove to be popular. After three performances it was not produced again until 1745, and then four years elapsed before it was to be heard again. Probably the reason for this lapse was the existence of a strong feeling among many people that a work so deeply religious should not be performed in a theater.

Janette Woolsey

GEORGE FREDERICK HANDEL
Unknown Artist
Scala/Art Resource, NY

Messiah

A Lost Chord

Seated one day at the Organ,
I was weary and ill at ease,
And my fingers wandered idly
Over the noisy keys.

I do not know what I was playing,
Or what I was dreaming then;
But I struck one chord of music,
Like the sound of a great Amen.

It flooded the crimson twilight
Like the close of an angel's psalm,
And it lay on my fevered spirit
With a touch of infinite calm.

It quieted pain and sorrow,
Like love overcoming strife;
It seemed the harmonious echo
From our discordant life.

It linked all perplexed meanings
Into one perfect peace,
And trembled away into silence,
As if it were loath to cease.

I have sought, but I seek it vainly,
That one lost chord divine,
That came from the soul of the Organ
And entered into mine.

It may be that Death's bright angel
Will speak in that chord again,
It may be that only in heaven
I shall hear that grand Amen.

Adelaide Anne Procter

ON APRIL 6, 1759, Handel directed *Messiah* for the last time in Covent Garden. For some years he had been in poor health, and his eyes were so bad that he was nearly blind. That evening after the performance he was taken ill, and during the night of Good Friday, April 13, 1759, George Frederick Handel died. He was buried in Westminster Abbey, and a statue of him marks the place of burial.

Although *Messiah* was never extremely popular during Handel's lifetime, it is without doubt the composition by which he is best remembered. It was first performed in the United States in New York City on January 16, 1770. In this performance *Messiah* was not given in its entirety, but in Boston on December 25, 1818, the whole oratorio was heard.

From this time it became traditional to give *Messiah* at Christmas. But in 1882, in Lindsborg, Kansas, it was performed at Eastertime. Everyone in the community took part—professional persons, laborers, housewives—all joined in. And once again the custom of giving it during the Easter season was established.

During the years which have followed its composing, *Messiah* seems more and more to express the true meaning of Easter. For it not only is the telling of the Old Testament prophecies of the coming of Christ, the Herald's announcing His birth and then Christ's life on earth, but the real meaning of the Crucifixion and Resurrection is finally summed up in an expression of man's faith in all that for which Christ stands.

Janette Woolsey

I Know That My Redeemer Liveth

Music by George Frederick Handel

He Shall Feed His Flock

From *Messiah* by George Frederick Handel

He Shall Feed His Flock

Lilies of Easter

nd why take ye thought for raiment? Consider the lilies of the field, how they grow; they toil not, neither do they spin: And yet I say unto you, That even Solomon in all his glory was not arrayed like one of these. . . . But seek ye first the kingdom of God, and his righteousness; and all these things shall be added unto you. Take therefore no thought for the morrow: for the morrow shall take thought for the things of itself. Sufficient unto the day is the evil thereof.

Matthew 6:28–29, 33–34

THE HISTORY of the Easter lily is a combination of both myth and symbol. Not only has the lily come to represent the renewal of life and rebirth of the spirit; it is also symbolic of innocence and purity.

The Easter lily with which we are most familiar is the *Lilium longiforum.* It is likely that this variety traveled from islands south of Japan to Bermuda where it flourished in the tropical climate. In North America it is widely grown in greenhouses for use at Easter. The Madonna Lily is the provincial flower of Quebec, Canada, perhaps because the bulbs of this variety come mainly from France. Our conventional Easter lily is cultivated primarily in the Pacific Northwest and California.

ACCORDING TO LEGEND, of all the flowers in the Garden of Gethsemane, the beautiful pure white lily was the most beautiful. The lily, however, was very aware of its great beauty and stood tall, its blossoms held high, to show itself to all who passed through the garden.

The night before He was to be crucified, Jesus came to the peaceful garden to pray. He prayed and He wept, causing all of the flowers of the garden to bow their heads in great pity and sorrow for Jesus. The pride-filled lily, however, did not bow its head.

On Good Friday, the lily learned that the sorrowing Jesus would die. In humiliation and anguish at its proud behavior of the night before, the lily now bowed its head in shame and sorrow. Since then the beautiful Easter lily remembers its sorrow by growing with down-turned blossoms.

The Lilly

The modest Rose
  puts forth a thorn;
The humble Sheep,
  a threat'ning horn;
While the Lilly white
  shall in Love delight;
Nor a thorn nor a threat
  stain her beauty bright.
    William Blake

EASTER LILIES AND PINK HYDRANGEA
Bellingrath Gardens, Theodore, Alabama
William H. Johnson/Johnson's Photography

A Prayer in Spring

Oh, give us pleasure in the flowers today;
And give us not to think so far away
As the uncertain harvest; keep us here
All simply in the springing of the year.

Oh, give us pleasure in the orchard white,
Like nothing else by day, like ghosts by night;
And make us happy in the happy bees,
The swarm dilating round the perfect trees.

And make us happy in the darting bird
That suddenly above the bees is heard,
The meteor that thrusts in with needle bill,
And off a blossom in mid air stands still.

For this is love and nothing else is love,
The which it is reserved for God above
To sanctify to what far ends He will,
But which it only needs that we fulfill.

Robert Frost

Thus We Come to Easter

EVER SINCE THE FIRST SPRING that ever was, man stood at this season with awe in his eyes and wonder in his heart, seeing the magnificence of life returning and life renewed. And something deep responded, whatever his religion or spiritual belief. It is as inevitable as sunrise that man should see the substance of faith and hope in the tangible world so obviously responding to forces beyond himself or his accumulated knowledge.

For all his learning and sophistication, man still instinctively reaches toward that force beyond, and thus approaches humility. Only arrogance can deny its existence, and the denial falters in the face of evidence on every hand. In every tuft of grass, in every bird, in every opening bud, there it is. We can reach so far with our explanations, and there still remains a force beyond which touches not only the leaf, the seed, the opening petal, but man himself.

Spring is a result, not a cause. The cause lies beyond, still beyond. And it is the instinctive knowledge of this which inspires our festivals of faith and life and belief renewed. Resurrection is there for us to witness and participate in; but the resurrection around us still remains the symbol, not the ultimate truth. And men of good will instinctively reach for truth—beyond the substance of spring, of a greening and revivifying earth, of nesting and mating and birth, of life renewed. Thus we come to Easter, and all the other festivals of faith, celebrating life and hope and the ultimate substance of belief—reaching, like the leaf itself, for something beyond, ever beyond.

Hal Borland

THE MUDDY RIVER AT
THE RIVERWAY
Boston, Massachusetts
Dick Dietrich/Dietrich Photography

EASTER
SYMBOLS
IN ART

I am the vine, ye

are the branches: He

that abideth in me,

and I in him, the

same bringeth forth

much fruit: for

without me ye can

do nothing.

John 15:5

LION The lion is used in Renaissance art with various meanings, depending upon the circumstances. In general, the lion is emblematic of strength, majesty, courage, and fortitude. Legendary natural history states that young lions are born dead, but come to life three days after birth when breathed upon by their sire. Thus, the lion has become associated with the Resurrection and is the symbol of Christ, the Lord of life.

ASPEN There are two early legends about the aspen tree. One relates that the cross was made from the aspen, and that, when the tree realized the purpose for which it was being used, its leaves began to tremble with horror and have never ceased. The other legend is that, as Christ died on the cross, all the trees bowed in sorrow except the aspen. Because of its pride and sinful arrogance, the leaves of the aspen were doomed to continual trembling.

DANDELION One of the "bitter herbs," the dandelion was used as a symbol of the Passion, and as such it appears, among other flowers, in paintings of the Madonna and Child, and of the Crucifixion.

GOURD The gourd is prominent in the story of Jonah, and because of this association with him has come to symbolize the Resurrection (Jonah 4). When painted together with an apple, the gourd, as the symbol of the Resurrection, is the antidote for the apple, the symbol of evil, or death. The gourd was used by pilgrims as a flask to carry water. It is the special attribute of James the Great, and of the Archangel Raphael, and is sometimes given to Christ, who, dressed as a pilgrim, joined the two Apostles on their way to Emmaus. Frequently, in art the gourd resembles a cucumber.

EAGLE The eagle may generally be interpreted as a symbol of the Resurrection. This is based upon the early belief that the eagle, unlike other birds, periodically renewed its plumage and its youth by flying near the sun and then plunging into the water. This interpretation is further borne out by Psalm 103:5, "thy youth is renewed like the eagle's."

BUTTERFLY The butterfly is sometimes seen in paintings of the Virgin and Child, and is usually in the Child's hand. It is a symbol of the Resurrection of Christ. In a more general sense, the butterfly may symbolize the resurrection of all men. This meaning is derived from the three stages in its life as represented by the caterpillar, the chrysalis, and the butterfly, which are clearly symbols of life, death, and resurrection.

EGG The egg is the symbol of hope and resurrection. This meaning is derived from the manner in which the small chick breaks from the egg at its birth.

GRAPES Bunches of grapes with ears of grain were sometimes used to symbolize the wine and bread of the Last Supper, or Communion. In general, the grape is a symbol of Christ. Representations of labor in the vineyards sometimes signify the work of good Christians in the vineyard of the Lord; the grape vine or leaf is used as an emblem of the Saviour, the "true vine."

George Ferguson

Turn your eyes

upon Jesus,

Look full in His

wonderful face,

And the things of

earth will grow

strangely dim

In the light of His

glory and grace.

Helen H. Lemmel

MERLOT GRAPES
Stockman/International Stock

The Easter Lamb

The next day John seeth Jesus coming unto him, and saith, Behold the Lamb of God, which taketh away the sin of the world. This is he of whom I said, After me cometh a man which is preferred before me: for he was before me. And I knew him not: but that he should be made manifest to Israel, therefore am I come baptizing with water. And John bare record, saying, I saw the Spirit descending from heaven like a dove, and it abode upon him. And I knew him not: but he that sent me to baptize with water, the same said unto me, Upon whom thou shalt see the Spirit descending, and remaining on him, the same is he which baptizeth with the Holy Ghost. And I saw, and bare record that this is the Son of God.

John 1:29–34

THE LITTLE LAMBS on Easter cards, toy lambs, and lambs made of candy or pastry go back far beyond Easter to the first Passover of the Jewish people.

It was at the time their ancestors were slaves in Egypt. Before the angel of God took the firstborn in all Egyptian homes, the Hebrew leader Moses ordered a sacrifice. Every Hebrew family was to sprinkle the blood of a young lamb over its doorframe. The lamb had to be roasted and eaten, together with bread baked without yeast, and bitter herbs. If this was done, Moses said, the angel would pass over their homes, and bring them no harm.

Hebrew people who joined the Christian religion in its early years brought with them the traditions of their ancient Passover festival. One of these was the sacrifice of a lamb. Gradually, as some of the older ways blended with the Christian customs, the lamb took on a different meaning. In the Hebrew religion, the lamb's life was a sacrifice to God. To the Christians, Jesus became the sacrificial lamb. The lamb became an Easter lamb, a symbol of Jesus.

The Lamb

Little lamb, who made thee?
 Dost thou know who made thee?
Gave thee life and bade thee feed,
By the stream and o'er the mead;
Gave thee clothing of delight,
Softest clothing, woolly, bright;
Gave thee such a tender voice,
Making all the vales rejoice?
 Little lamb, who made thee?
 Dost thou know who made thee?

Little lamb, I'll tell thee,
 Little lamb, I'll tell thee:
He is callèd by thy name,
For He calls Himself a Lamb.
He is meek and He is mild;
He became a little child.
I a child and thou a lamb.
We are callèd by His name.
 Little lamb, God bless thee!
 Little lamb, God bless thee!
 William Blake

Poems, stories, and hymns often call Jesus The Lamb of God. But sometimes he is The Good Shepherd with mankind as his flock. Many pictures show Jesus with a shepherd's staff, carrying a little lamb.

Besides its religious meaning, the Easter lamb had other meanings given to it by shepherds and farmers in earlier days. They believed it was good luck to meet a lamb, particularly during the Easter season. If you looked from your window on Easter Sunday and saw a lamb, you could expect even better luck, especially if its nose happened to be pointing toward your house. The reason given was that the devil could take any form but that of a dove or a lamb.

 Edna Barth

THE DEPOSITION OF JESUS CHRIST
Stefano Pieri
Accademia, Florence, Italy
Alinari/Art Resource, NY

Symbols of Christ and the Book of Kells

And I saw a strong angel proclaiming with a loud voice, Who is worthy to open the book, and to loose the seals thereof? And no man in heaven, nor in earth, neither under the earth, was able to open the book, neither to look thereon. And I wept much, because no man was found worthy to open and to read the book, neither to look thereon. And one of the elders saith unto me, Weep not: behold, the Lion of the tribe of Juda, the Root of David, hath prevailed to open the book, and to loose the seven seals thereof. And I beheld, and, lo, in the midst of the throne and of the four beasts, and in the midst of the elders, stood a Lamb as it had been slain, having seven horns and seven eyes, which are the seven Spirits of God sent forth into all the earth. And he came and took the book out of the right hand of him that sat upon the throne. And when he had taken the book, the four beasts and four and twenty elders fell down before the Lamb, having every one of them harps, and golden vials full of odours, which are the prayers of saints. And they sung a new song, saying, Thou art worthy to take the book, and to open the seals thereof: for thou wast slain, and hast redeemed us to God by thy blood out of every kindred, and tongue, and people, and nation.

Revelation 5:2–9

THE BOOK OF KELLS is considered to be the most lavishly decorated of a series of Gospel manuscripts produced between the seventh and ninth centuries. Whether or not the manuscript was actually written and illuminated at the Columban monastic community in the ancient town of Kells, Ireland, is an unsettled question. The earliest reference associating the book with Kells appears in the Annals of Ulster for the year 1006. There it records that the Gospels were stolen from the church at Kells and subsequently found several months later buried in a peat bog. Since 1661, the manuscript has been the chief treasure of the University Library at Trinity College in Dublin, where it is seen by thousands of people who take the opportunity to see the few pages that are selected for viewing during the course of the year.

The face of Christ is a constant figure in the Book of Kells. His face is often seen in the context of other symbols, most often with the figure of a fish. For the most part, Christ is represented as young and is often accompanied by not only the fish, but the lion, snake, and peacock.

Beginning in the second century, the fish was used as a symbol for Christ. The snake was a symbol of Christ's Resurrection, the meaning derived from the belief that a snake renewed its youth when it shed its skin. The snake is also a reminder of the fall of man and the loss of innocence.

The lion was yet another powerful symbol of Christ's Resurrection. There are many references in the Old Testament and also in the mythology of other cultures that portray the majesty and power of lions. This association links the lion to the royal house of Judah, from which Christ was descended.

Christ's incorruptibility was symbolized by the peacock, which was an emblem of eternity and divinity. According to an ancient belief, a peacock's flesh was so strong that it could not decay. In the Book of Kells, peacocks were often contorted into shapes which formed letters. These were frequently combined with a chalice and vines.

EIGHT-CIRCLE CROSS FROM THE BOOK OF KELLS MANUSCRIPTS
Trinity College, Dublin, Ireland
Bridgeman Art Library, London/SuperStock

PAGE FROM THE BOOK OF KELLS MANUSCRIPTS
Trinity College, Dublin, Ireland
ET Archive, London/SuperStock

The Fabergé Egg

ONE OF THE EGG-DECORATING STYLES most popular with home craftsmen is the Fabergé style. The modern imitations are often fashioned
from artificial gems and decorated with gilt, whereas the Russian
jeweler for whom they are named used genuine materials to create
ornate, jewel-encrusted eggs.

FABERGÉ EGG
Karl Fabergé
Christie's Images/SuperStock

Fabergé worked at the turn of the twentieth century. In Tsarist
Russia, Easter was one of the most important holidays of the year.
In addition to its religious significance, it was a time during which
families gathered, hospitality was extended to friends, and pres-
ents were exchanged. Decorated eggs were popular Easter gifts.
Those who could afford them, especially the Imperial family and
higher nobility, called on Karl Fabergé to make his superbly craft-
ed eggs.

Karl seems to have been raised to follow in the footsteps of his
father, who was a St. Petersburg jeweler. He had his first training
from the goldsmith Peter Pendin and also studied at a business
school in Dresden.

At the age of twenty-four, after a tour of Europe which included a
stay in Paris, young Karl took over his father's business. The stay in
France seems to have permanently affected him and his art. His jewelry,
fashioned after the French style of the eighteenth century, appealed to
the sophisticated residents of St. Petersburg.

Under Karl's management, the Fabergé firm expanded and began to
produce objects of fantasy along with the conventional jewelry which
had been the mainstay of the father's firm. It was by virtue of these inno-
vations that Karl's reputation grew in Europe as well as in Russia.
Eventually the firm opened branches in Kiev and Odessa and a retail out-
let in London. Each branch employed several craftsmen.

Fabergé soon attracted the attention of the royal family of Russia.
After the murder of Tsar Alexander II in 1881, the Tsarina Maria
Fyodorovna became terribly depressed. Her husband, Tsar Alexander III,

sought some way to cheer her up. He commissioned Fabergé to make her a present. The result was an exquisite Easter egg, which delighted the Tsarina.

The tradition was continued with Tsar Alexander's son and successor, Nicholas. Each year he gave a Fabergé egg to his wife and to his mother. Both eggs were kept secret until Easter morning.

The idea of giving decorated eggs at Easter did not originate with Alexander. It was customary for members of the royal household and the higher nobility to exchange them. But the eggs of Fabergé were special. The workmanship was extraordinary and intricate. The settings of precious stones harmonized perfectly with the total design. Inside the egg there was usually a surprise such as jewelry or some other gift, also made by Fabergé. In other eggs there were scenes from Russian life or miniatures of members of the royal family.

Fabergé and his craftsmen worked mainly in gold and silver. They were masters of the art of enameling. Enameled panels were often out-

THE PINECONE EGG
Karl Fabergé
Christie's Images/SuperStock

lined in pearls or diamonds. Many subjects besides miniature portraits were considered suitable for painting on eggs, and these were also set off by pearls, diamonds, or precious stones. Other popular materials were emerald, quartz, aquamarine, and ruby matrix.

During and after the Russian Revolution, most Fabergé eggs were taken out of the country. Many of them found their way into private American collections and museums where they are enjoyed today.

From Peasants to Kings: Pisanki Eggs

THE EASTER FEAST IN POLAND is probably the most complete and elaborate served in all the countries that celebrate Easter. First, the table itself is decorated with foliage. A lamb made of sugar, or a cake made in a lamb-shaped mold, dominates the center of the table. Around the figure of the lamb are placed platters of ham, sausages, cold roast pork, various kinds of salads, a dish of horseradish, and vinegar as a reminder of Christ's suffering on the cross and the vinegar He was given in response to His cry "I thirst." The lamb symbol is repeated again in the mold of butter. There is also a loaf of high-rising *babka* bread, and *chrusciki,* Polish love knots. On a china plate (the very best china is used on this special day) are replicas, in miniature, of all the main dishes, fashioned out of colored marzipan.

Of great importance to this feast is the display of Easter eggs, *pisanki* (or *pysanky*), as they are called. As famed for it as for their cooking, the Polish people excel in Easter egg decoration and, together with the Ukrainians, are the acknowledged masters of this particular art. Hours upon hours go into a single decoration, which may be of a geometrical or abstract pattern. Christian symbols such as the fish and the cross are also used. To produce such superbly decorated eggs requires not only patience and skill, but also native ability and technical know-how. To the blown egg, wax is applied by means of a needle or a tiny metal tube. Sometimes the tip of a shoelace is used. Parts of the egg are coated with the wax so that they will not absorb color when the eggs are dipped into a particular dye. To achieve the multicolored effect, the egg is waxed and dipped repeatedly. Each color has its own particular source. To get the most delicate light green shade, one must use moss that has been taken from underneath a stone. An infusion of crocuses supplies the orange tone, and black is brewed from alder bark and cones. These eggs are presented as gifts and are always kept for a long time.

Easter eggs are not usually given to one's parents or children; rather, these special gifts are presented to godparents and to friends. A gift of an Easter egg from a young lady to a young man is a sign that his attentions will not be unwelcome. In years gone by, Polish girls gave their favored suitors anywhere from thirty to a hundred eggs, which they decorated themselves; or, if they were not skilled in the art, they patronized women who were. If the girl had to "purchase" her eggs, she might perform housekeeping chores, thus releasing the artist for egg-making. When the eggs were finished, the young lady, eager to please her suitor, wrapped the eggs carefully in a fine lawn handkerchief, tucked in a handful of nuts and a packet of tobacco, and offered the gift to her chosen one. He was expected to reciprocate with a piece of dress material, a kerchief, ribbons of many colors, or all three! This customary gift-giving is now fading into the past.

PISANKI EGGS
Arthur/Mauritius/
H. Armstrong Roberts

Several legends and cherished beliefs surround the Easter eggs and their importance in the life of the Poles. One of the fables concerning the presence of *pisanki* at the Easter table relates to Mary Magdalene. She and her companions went to the sepulcher with sweet spices with which to anoint Christ's body and took a few cooked eggs with them in a basket to eat after they had completed this sad mission. On their arrival at Christ's tomb, they found that their eggs had miraculously taken on all the colors of the rainbow. Another tale relates that the first *pisanki* were made by Mary, the mother of Jesus, in the peaceful days at Nazareth, long before the shadows of Calvary fell across her life. To amuse the infant Jesus, she took eggs from her household store and boiled them until they were hard. She then painted them red and green and yellow.

The *pisanki* are thought to have the power of protecting the house from all evil. Always a few of them are kept, since they will bring good luck to the house. A few are planted in the vineyard to guard the vines against hail, wind, and destructive storms.

Stronger than the dark,
the light;
Stronger than the wrong,
the right;
Faith and hope
triumphant say
Christ will rise on
Easter Day.
Phillips Brooks

Maker of Heaven and Earth

All things bright and beautiful,
    All creatures great and small,
All things wise and wonderful,
    The Lord God made them all.

Each little flower that opens,
    Each little bird that sings,
He made their glowing colors,
    He made their tiny wings.

The rich man in his castle,
    The poor man at his gate,
God made them, high or lowly,
    And ordered their estate.

The purple-headed mountain,
    The river running by,
The sunset, and the morning
    That brightens up the sky,

The cold wind in the winter,
    The pleasant summer sun,
The ripe fruits in the garden,
    He made them every one.

The tall trees in the green wood,
    The meadows where we play,
The rushes by the water,
    We gather every day—

He gave us eyes to seem them,
    And lips that we might tell,
How great is God Almighty,
    Who has made all things well.
        Cecil Frances Alexander

SUNRISE OVER THE GRAND TETONS
Grand Teton National Park, Wyoming
Osolinki/FPG International

The Cherry-Tree Carol

Joseph was an old man,
 And an old man was he,
And he married Mary,
 The Queen of Galilee.

Joseph and Mary walked
 Through an orchard good,
Where was cherries and berries,
 As red as any blood.

Joseph and Mary walked
 Through an orchard green,
Where was berries and cherries,
 As thick as might be seen.

Oh, then bespoke Mary,
 So meek and so mild;
"Pluck me one cherry, Joseph,
 For I am with child."

Oh, then bespoke Joseph
 With words most unkind:
"Let Him pluck thee a cherry
 That brought thee with child."

Oh, then bespoke the Babe,
 Within His mother's womb:
"Bow down then the tallest tree,
 For My mother to have some."

Then bowed down the highest tree
 Unto His mother's hand;
Then she cried: "See, Joseph,
 I have cherries at command."

Oh, then bespake Joseph:
 "I have done Mary wrong;
But cheer up, my dearest,
 And be not cast down."

Then Mary plucked a cherry,
 As red as the Blood;
Then Mary went home
 With her heavy load.

Then Mary took her Babe,
 And sat Him on her knee,
Saying: "My dear Son, tell me
 What this world will be."

"Oh, I shall be as dead, Mother,
 As the stones in the wall;
Oh, the stones in the streets, Mother,
 Shall mourn for Me all.

"Upon Easter-day, Mother,
 My uprising shall be;
Oh, the sun and the moon, Mother,
 Shall both rise with Me."
 Author Unknown

CHERRY TREES IN BLOOM AROUND THE TIDAL BASIN
Washington, D.C.
William Johnson/Johnson's Photography

On the Road to Emmaus

And, behold, two of them went that same day to a village called Emmaus, which was from Jerusalem about threescore furlongs. And they talked together of all these things which had happened. And it came to pass, that, while they communed together and reasoned, Jesus himself drew near, and went with them. But their eyes were holden that they should not know him. . . . And he went in to tarry with them. And it came to pass, as he sat at meat with them, he took bread, and blessed it, and brake, and gave to them. And their eyes were opened, and they knew him; and he vanished out of their sight.

Luke 24:13–16, 29–31

The Walk to Emmaus

Late on that afternoon
Two men walked down Emmaus way.
A Traveler drew near and asked,
"Why are ye sorrowful this day?"

They told Him of their Lord, condemned
Three days before, and crucified,
Yet Who arose. "How can this be?"
They asked the Stranger, close beside.

He held them spellbound on the road,
As He explained the Scriptures then:
Of how God sent His Son to die,
And on the third day rise again.

At dusk they reached Emmaus, still
And peaceful in the countryside.

"The day is now far spent," they said,
"Come in and with us here abide."

And He went in that twilight hour
And sat at meat there with the two;
And as He broke and blessed the bread,
Their eyes were opened, and they knew!

Then, lo, He vanished from their sight,
And each exclaimed with one accord,
"Did not our hearts burn as He talked?
It was the Lord—our Blessed Lord!"

Immediately they rose with joy
And ran back to Jerusalem,
Telling that Jesus was alive,
And that they had communed with Him.
William Arnette Wofford

SPRINGTIME MEADOW
Mt. Baker, Washington
Terry Donnelley/Tony Stone Images

Worthy Is the Lamb

And I beheld, and I heard the voice of many angels round about the throne and the beasts and the elders: and the number of them was ten thousand times ten thousand, and thousands of thousands; Saying with a loud voice, Worthy is the Lamb that was slain to receive power, and riches, and wisdom, and strength, and honour, and glory, and blessing. And every creature which is in heaven, and on the earth, and under the earth, and such as are in the sea, and all that are in them, heard I saying, Blessing, and honour, and glory, and power, be unto him that sitteth upon the throne, and unto the Lamb for ever and ever.

Revelation 5:11–13

Peace I leave with you, my peace I give unto you: not as the world giveth, give I unto you. Let not your heart be troubled, neither let it be afraid.

Ye have heard how I said unto you, I go away, and come again unto you. If ye loved me, ye would rejoice, because I said, I go unto the Father: for my Father is greater than I.

And now I have told you before it come to pass, that, when it is come to pass, ye might believe.

John 14:27–29

Ascension

It happens through the blond window, the trees
With diverse leaves divide the light, light birds;
Aeengus, the god of Love, my shoulders brushed
With birds, you could say lark or thrush or thieves

And not be right yet—or ever right—
For it was God's Son foreign to our moor;
When I looked out the window, all was white,
And what's beloved in the heart was sure,

With such a certainty ascended He,
That Son of Man who deigned Himself to be,
That when we lifted out of sleep, there was
Life with its dark, and love above the laws.

Denis Devlin

INTERIOR OF A CHURCH
Minneapolis, Minnesota
Bob Firth/International Stock

With Sorrow and True Repentance

*I*n a moment, in the twinkling of an eye, at the last trump: for the trumpet shall sound, and the dead shall be raised incorruptible, and we shall be changed. For this corruptible must put on incorruption, and this mortal must put on immortality. So when this corruptible shall have put on incorruption, and this mortal shall have put on immortality, then shall be brought to pass the saying that is written, Death is swallowed up in victory. O death, where is thy sting? O grave, where is thy victory? The sting of death is sin; and the strength of sin is the law. But thanks be to God, which giveth us the victory through our Lord Jesus Christ.

1 Corinthians 15:52–57

FORGIVE ME, Lord Jesus, for the things that I have done that make me feel uncomfortable in Thy presence. All the front that I polish so carefully for men to see, does not deceive Thee.

For Thou knowest every thought that has left its shadow on my memory. Thou hast marked every motive that curdled something sweet within me.

I acknowledge, with sorrow and true repentance, that I have desired that which I should not have; I have toyed with what I knew was not for me; I have been preoccupied with self-interest; I have invited unclean thoughts into my mind and entertained them as honored guests; my ears have often been deaf to Thy whisper; my eyes have often been blind to the signs of Thy guidance. Make me willing to be changed, even though it requires surgery of the soul, and therapy of discipline.

Make my heart warm and soft, that I may receive and accept now the blessing of Thy forgiveness, the benediction of Thy "Depart in peace . . . and sin no more." In Jesus' name. Amen.

Peter Marshall

THE SEINE AT NOTRE DAME
C. T. Guillermot
Waterhouse and Dodd,
London/Bridgeman Art Library,
London/SuperStock

The Hound of Heaven

I fled Him, down the nights and down the days;
I fled Him, down the arches of the years;
I fled Him, down the labyrinthine ways
Of my own mind; and in the midst of tears
I hid from Him, and under running laughter
Up vistaed hopes I sped;
And shot, precipitated
Down Titanic glooms of chasmed fears,
From those strong Feet that followed, followed after.
But with unhurrying chase,
And unperturbed pace,
Deliberate speed, majestic instancy,
They beat—and a Voice beat
More instant than the Feet—
"All things betray thee, who betrayest Me. . . .
Whom wilt thou find to love ignoble thee
Save Me, save only Me?
All which I took from thee, I did but take,
Not for thy harms,
But just that thou might'st seek it in My arms.
All which thy child's mistake
Fancies as lost, I have stored for thee at home;
Rise, clasp My hand, and come!"
Halts by me that footfall:
Is my gloom, after all,
Shade of His hand, outstretched caressingly?
"Ah, fondest, blindest, weakest,
I am He Whom thou seekest!
Thou dravest love from thee, who dravest Me."

Francis Thompson

INDEX